HENRY FORD
and
GREENFIELD VILLAGE

By
WILLIAM ADAMS SIMONDS

Profusely Illustrated

FREDERICK A. STOKES COMPANY
NEW YORK   MCMXXXVIII

Printed in the United States of America

● Martha-Mary Chapel, Greenfield Village. Named for the mothers of Mr. and Mrs. Henry Ford.

To
PAT
AND
BETTY

CONTENTS

LIST OF ILLUSTRATIONS

LIST OF ILLUSTRATIONS

x

LIST OF ILLUSTRATIONS

FOREWORD

*T*EN YEARS AGO WHEN
I wrote a book about the life of Henry Ford, I
called him a "motor genius," because that expression seemed to describe most aptly his
career and achievements in the field of mass
production and industry. By the world at large,
he has been regarded as one of its greatest industrialists, producer of millions of automobiles and employer of thousands of men. Today
he still occupies that position.

During the decade that has elapsed since that
book appeared, an important new activity has
been created by the "motor genius" which,
many predict, will perpetuate his memory long
after his automobiles and machines have been
forgotten. It has taken place in his home city
of Dearborn, the town of his boyhood, about
twelve miles west of the metropolis of Detroit.
Here on the banks of the winding Rouge River,

not far from the spot where that stream flows through the grounds of his home and within sight of the smokestacks of the vast Rouge plant, he has brought into being an educational project, a memorial to his friend Thomas Alva Edison. With its schools, its early American village, and its historical museum, this new creation has become the mecca of literally millions of visitors from every part of the globe.

This is true, even though the project is not yet completed, nor will be for several years to come. Nearly every day sees some new change introduced, a progressive step adding to its value and serving to round out the whole. Mr. Ford believes in change, and for that reason many of the matters herein described as brand-new will have become history, or will have been improved by new factors, even before this book leaves the publisher's hands.

As founder and president of the Edison Institute, Mr. Ford naturally continues to devote much of his time to its development.

WILLIAM ADAMS SIMONDS

Dearborn,
Michigan.

xiv

HENRY FORD
and
GREENFIELD
VILLAGE

Chapter I

TAKING TIME

I

RECENTLY TWO
young men from a West Coast high school arrived at Dearborn to present to Mr. Henry
Ford a copy of their student year-book, which
their class had dedicated to him, and to obtain
his autograph for a copy that was to be deposited in the school library. After he had
chatted with them for perhaps half an hour, he
rose to leave. One of them remarked, "Gee,
Mr. Ford! It's certainly been generous of you
to give us so much time!" Smilingly he replied, "Well, boys, if I'm not able *now* to take
time to do the things I want to do, I never will
be."

Visitors at Dearborn—and their total is nearly
a million a year—frequently comment on the
attention he has paid in late years to the de-

3

velopment of a closer link between industry, education and agriculture. They apparently expect that a man of such far-flung, important enterprises can have little time for ideas seemingly apart from his business of automobile manufacturing. When they learn that every morning he attends the chapel service of the Greenfield Village school children, that he personally directs every detail of the Village, that he spends many days in the country where soybeans are being grown and century-old gristmills are being restored for productive use, that in other localities over the United States— at Wayside Inn in Massachusetts, at Ways, Georgia, and on the Upper Peninsula of Michigan—he is directing educational experiments linking agriculture and industry to the training of youth, they profess surprise.

Often a visitor remarks, "I've received an entirely different glimpse of Mr. Ford. Heretofore, I have always associated him with mass production and the providing of low-cost transportation. How do you explain this change?"

The fact of the matter is that what Mr. Ford has been giving reality to during the past ten

4

years had been in his mind for many years before. Germinating and coming to bud, the
ideas are now in bloom. More than most men,
he is infinitely patient and willing to make
progress slowly. He has followed the admoni-
tion of Longfellow as expressed in a verse he
often quotes:

"Still achieving, still pursuing,
Learn to labor, and to wait."

Mr. Ford sees no reason why industry should
be apart from other large interests in American
life. He believes that it should concern itself
with the education of our young, not alone in
technical schools, but even in the primary and
intermediate grades. He looks upon industry,
agriculture and education as cooperating, rather
than as separate worlds each intent on its own
concerns.

There is nothing secret about his ideas or his
methods in working them out. They are open
to the world and particularly to the industrial
world; they may be taken and applied anywhere. Nothing would give him more genuine
pleasure than to find other industrial leaders
joining him in furthering such a program.

5

As long ago as 1929, in an interview he said:*

"The finding and developing of leaders is the greatest need of the country today. . . . What is wrong with the young people in this country, if anything, is merely that older people, and especially men who have risen to positions of large responsibility, don't take sufficient interest in the young folks . . . don't try to find out what stuff is in those youngsters and try to develop it.

"Our life has become altogether too complex to yield the necessary training out of books alone. The boys have got to know a lot about everything these days in order to know any single thing well. And that is especially true of the industrial activities of the country, which have assumed such immense proportions.

"Can you imagine a boy going through school with no interest except getting his marks out of his books, and being really prepared to do any original creative work in the world? I can't. Unless the lad has been prying into a lot of the materials and processes that enter into our complex life, examining everything and

---

* From North American Newspaper Alliance, August 18, 1929.

6

questioning everything, he is little better fitted after school training than he was before to have an active share in practical American life. . . .

"The country is simply crying for qualified leaders of the right type. We must get them out of the youth of the country. It can't be done without some real effort and attention to the need. We must teach boys to open their eyes . . . never to pass over a brick on the road without trying to learn something about it.

"I believe in mixing the old with the young. The generations should mingle. When I was a young man all my friends were old men . . . they had everything to teach me. There is a way for older men to be of help to younger, and when this becomes widespread we will have found more than a few bright boys—we will have discovered a bright up-and-coming generation."

One month after this appeared in print, through his efforts the first school in Greenfield Village was opened to younger pupils.

II

At the outset it should be clear that no one claims there is anything new in his ideas, unless it be the desire to recover such things from the past as are valuable. He has described his ideas on education as "the McGuffey type." His creation of the early American Village and Museum was designed to emphasize the pioneer qualities of self-dependence and resourcefulness that carved this country from a wilderness. His linking of agriculture and industry traces back to colonial days when every farmer had a side line, a winter occupation as well as a season of producing crops.

Nor is there anything new about his interest in young people. In girls it is as sincere and deep-rooted as in boys. To many, his understanding with very young children is the most surprising thing of all. Yet to observe it is not more surprising than the manner in which the very little ones respond. Instinctively they turn to him as to an old friend. With them as with his highest executives, as with critical in-

8

terviewers or the most common broom-pusher, he is always natural.

His interest in young people is based on the knowledge that tomorrow they will rule the world. When the former Mrs. Edison and he were discussing plans for the Edison Institute, she asked: "How do you intend to endow it, Mr. Ford?" With a quizzical smile, he answered: "With youth." That cryptic remark has puzzled more than one inquirer, but those who have stood on the sidelines and have watched the development of the Institute during the past ten years are beginning to see what he had in mind.

Seven years ago (July, 1931) he said in *The American Boy:*

"Boys sometimes ask me if there is room for them in the world. It seems to them that all the places are taken, all the jobs filled. But if they will think of the lines of business that did not exist a generation ago they will see that they have a thousand opportunities where the boys of their fathers' generation had but one. And if they will look around and see the thousand other lines of progress waiting to be

9

developed, they will see that opportunities increase faster than men can seize them and use them.

"The world wants more brains, more energy, more service, more vision all the time, and only youth can supply these.

"It is easier for boys to get started now. Big industry has gathered the instruments out of which a new world can be built. It used to take a century for an idea to gain acceptance, now it can go around the world in an hour and prove itself in a year or two. Yes, this is a better time to be young than any time that has preceded it."

In line with the purpose of education for leadership is the development of a wider range of interest in the child. Visitors who get behind the scenes at Dearborn are amazed at the sight of six-year-old youngsters learning to operate typewriters, of twelve-year-old boys learning to use lathes, of high school girls at a telephone switchboard or performing actual service in a stenographic department.

Small tots weave at looms specially designed for them, or wield miniature hoes between rows

10

of vegetables in garden tracts prepared for them. As they grow older they stand before microphones and participate in broadcasts over a nationwide network. Young or old take part equally in operettas or playlets on a modern stage. Camera study is as important as algebra; repairing of automobiles or radios, shopping for supper or preparing a menu, is as much a part of the curriculum as chemistry.

Behind these activities is the belief that thus will be made apparent the one interest which is to dominate the child's life. That is not always possible where the interests are few, or of one kind. Studies in books may leave unopened a whole world wherein the child's undeveloped interests may lie. By throwing open a wide variety, Mr. Ford expects to avoid that narrowness and provide each with an opportunity to make his or her natural choice of work. The more things a child can know about, the more things he can be initiated into doing, the greater the probability he will find a work which will most usefully employ his powers through life, and provide the most satisfaction.

No door in the vast Ford organization is

11

closed to these children. They freely explore, asking questions as to how and why, talking with men actually on the job, acquainting themselves with the mysteries of manufacture and service. Eventually they will specialize, but only after they have obtained a general knowledge that makes them better able to determine the field in which to specialize.

Nor is all this one-sided. He believes that older people may learn "infinitely more than they imagine" from children. He does not credit parents with having as much influence over their children as the children have over their parents. Parents who do not seize every possible opportunity to be with their children do not know what they are missing. Anyone who spends time with children is infinitely better for it. Lucky indeed is the grown-up whom children like.

In one of the talks I have had with him, he said: "All industry is education. Some men teach others how to do things. I made my first car myself, then had to teach others.

"I hope to interest industry in education. Here is a wide field that industry has over-

12

looked. I don't mean the technical school, I mean the training of our future market. We must give it some thought."

He quoted from a McGuffey Reader:

"The lark is up to meet the sun,
 The bee is on the wing;
The ant its labor has begun,
 The woods with music ring.

"Shall birds and bees and ants be wise,
 While I my moments waste?
O let me with the morning rise
 And to my duty haste."

He added with a smile: "My grandson wanted to replace the word 'duty' with 'work.' I said 'All right,' but the verse didn't sound right."

Later he referred to an incident in one of the Village schools. An older girl pupil had been called in to help the teacher of a lower grade. When she left to go back to her own classes, she said she had learned more than the children.

III

At his time of life—in July, 1938, he will round out three-quarters of a century—the

13

thoughts of most persons turn to the past, lin-
gering on memories of days and happiness gone
by.   Here again he differs from so many.   He
thinks only in terms of the present and the
future.   Although the foremost collector of
early Americana and the creator of an old-time
village, his objective has not been to preserve
these as a collector—rather for the use of present and future generations.   Some one has
called it "Looking forward through the past."
He himself has said, "The farther you look
back, the farther you can look ahead."

He does not worry about the future.   In all
his chats, this characteristic shines like a golden
thread—complete faith in America's future, in
the ultimate triumph of right, in the destiny
and pioneer spirit of the American people.

Part of his creed is based on the belief that
man is on the earth to gain experience, and
that this is not confined to earth alone.   Once
when asked to name the greatest happening of
the past half-century, he answered that it was
Thomas Alva Edison's conclusion that there
was an existence beyond death.   Conceptions
of the hereafter vary.   Mr. Ford's might be

14

said to include an evolution onward and upward, in which millions of opportunities for new experiences await us.

"It has taken a long time to bring us up to where we are," he told B. C. Forbes,* "but we will go on and on until we can create things now utterly beyond our ken." He added, "What we call death doesn't end all for us, by any means."

So, when Meigs O. Frost asked him on his seventy-first birthday: "Mr. Ford, nobody lives forever. I should like to ask you what plans you have made for the continuation of your business after your death?" Mr. Ford answered: "What the devil can I do about it? I'm not thinking about that at all. I have enough to do today." †

The world has heard often of the vast enterprise he has created in the field of industry, and of his tremendous responsibilities. Of the thousands employed by him, he seems most free of responsibilities. No one works longer hours or covers more ground, yet he seems to

---

* September 1, 1929, *Forbes Magazine.*
† New Orleans *Times Picayune,* July, 1934.

15

have time to chat with children, to observe nature, to talk with workmen, unhurried and unworried. People who have no time, don't think, he once said. The more you think, the more time you have.

On one occasion when I sought him for a decision on some matter which I have since forgotten, I found him standing by a window, alone. He seemed to be engrossed in thought and I turned to withdraw. He halted me. "Don't go," he said. "What is it?" I replied, "I don't want to interrupt you if you're thinking about something. I'll come back." He walked over from the window briskly. "I don't know whether I'm thinking or not," he said. "Sometimes it seems to me that when I'm thinking, I'm merely running up an antenna and waiting for thoughts to come in."

Again he said, speaking of church: "It always does a man good to step inside a church. Even if there isn't any service, just to step inside will do him good. No one could help getting a benefit merely by being in a place where so many good thoughts have been experienced."

16

In understanding what he seeks to do, and the developments he is today accomplishing, one must keep constantly in mind the accent on youth. His philosophy is not of the Horatio Alger type; rather it emphasizes work, experience, service, living. He predicts a reward for those who faithfully fulfil this program—not of money, for to him money is a tool to be used, not a reward—but of joy in the job, joy in creating, joy in leaving the world a better place.

Chapter II

EDUCATION FOR LIVING

I

*W*HAT ARE THE
objectives sought in the Ford educational program? Upon what fundamentals is it based,
and how do they differ from modern schooling
systems?

As already indicated, Mr. Ford claims nothing new for his ideas except, perhaps, their
resurrection from the past. The "McGuffey
type," as he has called it, refers to the one-room
school for the smaller grades where younger
children learn by listening to older ones, while
the latter learn consideration by associating
with, helping, and teaching the younger. In
such a program, smaller grades are essential.

More than one big-city educator, with whom
I have discussed this, has pronounced it unfeasi-
ble for congested schools in thickly populated

areas, where mass education seems the only method. Mass education carries with it huge sprawling edifices and regimented instruction; neither has a place in the Ford program.

Yet small buildings and small classes for younger children, feeding to a larger high school, are not unknown or unusual in America. Though small, the buildings are strongly built, well furnished and completely comfortable, yet inexpensive. There are no heavy debts with interest hanging over taxpayers.

It might be described as a decentralization of education. If, as some educators have asserted, it will not prove practical in large cities, at least there is no such obstacle in smaller ones, or in rural areas. Within a radius of one hundred miles from Dearborn, Mr. Ford has reopened a number of district schools that had been closed. Their pupils, children of nearby farmers, had been riding to and from a large city on buses. Back now in the neighborhood district school, they receive the advantages of advanced modern instruction from traveling supervisors, who teach choral work, athletics, art, dancing, and similar subjects. In other

22

words, the teachers travel instead of the pupils.

In such schools, association between older and younger children is natural. At recess, the limited number makes it possible for even the little fellows to get a turn at bat. It is surprising to see how quickly they learn to paddle in the water, to master the steps of the quadrille.

Mr. Ford has summed it up: "Our schools here, some people say, are not city schools, I don't want them to be city schools, for I hope to teach our boys and girls to live in the America of tomorrow, which I think is going to be more rural than it has been for the past generation. There was a flow to the cities, and men learned a good deal about living together in cities—sanitation, order, and the like—but now the flow is away from them. The water that is up the river, and the water now going over the wheel, are of more importance to youngsters than water that already has gone out to sea."

His system has been built to benefit the child, rather than to fit the child into the system. It is molded on the child, and he freely admits that it has still a long way to go. As he once said, "We are beginning to suspect that

23

youth educates us as much as we educate youth."

II

More important than the reestablishment of the small school is the development of a wider range of interests in the child, of a many-sided expansion—the teaching of many ways to earn a livelihood. In this, Mr. Ford has drawn from his own long experience as an employer. He has found that there is not enough kinship between what a man knows, and what he can *do*. That is why he has said that he is not interested in a man's college degree until he finds what the man has done with it. He defines an educated person as one who not only knows a lot, but knows how to do a lot of things.

The objective toward which he would have Education direct its efforts is simply to become a vital part of a child's life. It has been looked upon as a way of preparing him to enter upon life. This viewpoint is wrong, Mr. Ford believes, because it leads the pupil to regard life and education as two separate things. He

24

would have education continue throughout life.

A properly educated person, in his opinion, is able to adjust himself to any and all situations, however unexpected. He will surmount a depression because he can do more than one thing.

It is never too early for the child to learn how to do something useful, and begin to earn something. Teaching the child to earn a living is an essential part of Mr. Ford's program, not merely to earn, but to live so that what is earned may signify something.

From his school the boy or girl would go smoothly into life without the sudden and violent jerk that has marked Commencement Day so often—the transition from learning to living. In his school the boy or girl while learning would learn about life, for the school would be like life, not different. Its activities would be much like those of earning a living. Its graduates, since they had learned how to do many things, would have definite ideas about what they wanted to do, and would be able to do them. Instead of knowing *about* things, they would know how to *do* things.

"It is a waste," said Mr. Ford, "to take years out of a child's life, then cut him free to roam a world he does not understand, to hunt for work which he must learn how to do."

Some one remarks: "That is all very well for a man like Mr. Ford to say, for he has at his disposal one of the world's largest industrial enterprises into which his pupils may fit. But how about the ordinary school system?"

Mr. Ford sees nothing in this part of his program that cannot be applied anywhere. Boys may learn to repair household equipment, from leaky faucets to noisy radios, in schools of any size, if the course is provided. Girls may learn to mend and to cook. Both boys and girls may commence at an early age to tend gardens on vacant lots, supplying food for the home table and selling the surplus. As they grow older and become more skilled in some particular field, their earning power naturally increases. A girl who is able to weave a bed coverlet or a luncheon set, tend a telephone switchboard or type letters, a boy who can operate a lathe or

26

read a blueprint, grow soybeans, or paint a barn, is in a position to earn more.

Such a program is an effective preventive for the suggestion that there is something disgraceful about having to earn a living. Its pupils have no envy of the man who has been taught, as Mr. Ford describes it, to make money "in a paper world."

Earning a living is an essential part of life; it should have a place in every educational system.

Individual effort and intelligence must be first trained before the community as a whole can prosper. The individual must be personally both competent and solvent before you can have a "planned economy." "There is," Mr. Ford believes, "no system of government and no scheme of life that can relieve you, individually, of the obligation to do your own task with discrimination."

Only after you have formed an acquaintance with how to do many things, will you be able to select a single thing on which to specialize. One man's trade may be another's hobby or a third's talent. But nobody knows this at the

27

outset, and Mr. Ford proposes to let it develop and prove itself. If a man has a bent it will show.

"The weakness of specialization is obvious," said Mr. Ford. "It works well only when the world is just so. Our task is to equip boys and girls to do many things, to live under a variety of conditions, under rapidly changing conditions, and to be quick to make adjustments to new conditions."

In other words, stay close to life.

III

Still a third fundamental in Mr. Ford's educational program is the stressing of conduct, and the forming of a reverent attitude toward life. This begins with the morning assembly in the chapel overlooking the green at Greenfield Village. Arriving from their homes in gray buses, the pupils young and old stream across the green to the red brick chapel with its white spire.

Built of bricks that once formed the walls of Mrs. Ford's girlhood home, it is named for

28

the mothers of Mr. and Mrs. Henry Ford—the Chapel of Martha-Mary. Non-sectarian, it has never been consecrated, nor is it in the usual sense of the term a "religious" edifice. As the children gather, occasionally laughter rings out, for there is nothing solemn or long-faced about the building. Often the recitations are about subjects far removed from serious meditation.

Baseball stars and motion picture comedians have spoken to the children from its chancel, as did Will Rogers and Herbert Hoover. But moral discussions also have their time and place. Often a recitation will point a moral, consciously or otherwise, or a speaker will dwell on the spiritual. Seth Parker and his Maine friends may conduct a song service; a noted author or composer may address the pupils.

Through it all the McGuffey influence is most apparent, a happy combination of fun and behavior. Some of their songs are from McGuffey's Readers. The young voices ring out:

> "Hear the children gaily shout,
> 'Half-past four, and school is out!' "

29

Or,

"On the cheerful village green,
    Scattered round with houses neat,
All the boys and girls are seen,
    Playing there with busy feet."

Interspersed among these McGuffey songs and the familiar ones of Stephen Collins Foster will be heard a Psalm recited in unison from memory, or the Ten Commandments or the Lord's Prayer sung in rhyme. There is no furtherance of creeds, and no transgression of creeds.

Thus the day begins for the pupils. Seated in the white pews of the colonial chapel, they forget their petty differences as the organ sounds an introduction to a familiar tune. It may be one from Gilbert and Sullivan, or it may be a recent cowboy chant. Or it may be an old church favorite, "I Love to Tell the Story." All are memorized.

Morning after morning, month after month, year upon year amid such surroundings will provide sustaining, guiding memories that will last a lifetime—exercising a beneficial influence on character and attitude toward life.

30

Coupled with the chapel service is the association between older and younger pupils. Mr. Ford believes that here also is a means of molding character. He is undisturbed at reports that Johnny Jones is bullying the smaller boys. The older boys will straighten Johnny out. And don't worry if little Mary Smith is copying another girl's answers. The older girls will take care of it.

An important element in proper development of conduct is happiness. The happy, active child is not only gaining experience, but is also building character. The pupils are taught to enjoy Nature. "When there is snow, play in it; when there is ice, skate on it. In the summer, swim in the lakes and ponds. Learn birds and trees and flowers and rocks. The finest pleasures are those we discover and develop ourselves."

Mr. Ford would regard his schools as failures if they turned out boys and girls "who had to buy all their recreations."

"The truths of life," said Mr. Ford, "should be stated simply, clearly, and often to children. Just the right truth, coming into a child's life

31

at the right time, may be of great use later on.
We cannot know when that right time is to arrive, so repetition is the safer course. A platitude is not a platitude the first time a child
hears it. To him it is a striking way of putting
a fact. 'What is worth doing at all is worth
doing well' is old stuff to us grown-ups, but
many of us have been saved by that principle of
conduct. We laugh at it now, but we can't
escape from the effect it had upon us when we
first heard it, and the effect it has had in actual
practice throughout our lives."

One discovers the emphasis on conduct in
unexpected places. Hot lunches are served the
pupils at noon, and at each table where four
are seated, a boy or a girl acts as host or hostess.
Their duty is to see that manners are good and
talk interesting. In the old-time dance classes,
certain deportment is stressed—the proper way
to address a girl, the proper way to conduct her
to her seat. No slipshod manners are tolerated.

Good conduct brings poise, patience, toler-
ance, understanding. A young man or young
woman with poise is more likely to land a job,
hold it and rise, than one who is awkward.

32

● When the first Village school opened in 1929, Henry Ford greeted the pupils.

● Schools of the entire county adjourn for day
so students may travel by special train to
Greenfield Village.

● McGuffey Log School, Greenfield Village.
Used by first and second grade classes.

IV

During the past decade, the years in which Greenfield Village schools have been in operation, we have seen important changes in their procedure. This has been easy to effect, since Mr. Ford regards nothing as fixed in the system. Whenever an experience shows how to get results more quickly, the methods are changed. The principles remain unchanged.

The proof of the value of any educational theory must wait until the generation which has been educated under it has arrived at full activity as bearers of the world's responsibilities. By that time, the educators are usually dead and the theory itself has given place to a new one.

The only test that can be applied to the theory is its power to produce a competent generation, and such a test has never been made. It takes too long.

About all we know about the "McGuffey type" of schooling of the Middle West was that it was in use when a very competent and honorable generation of Americans was being reared,

33

and it is reasonable to assume that this type had something to do with the quality of the men and women who passed through it. It put its pupils in possession of certain plain principles and gave them an elevated view of life; both of which were reflected in the character and attitude of two or three generations of Americans.

Later came another system of education with improved teaching methods, perhaps, but with a decided decrease in emphasis on moral principles. Some have even suggested that there may be a connection between this system and the superficial, loose and bewildered generation that came out of it.

It may be possible, of course, that the worst educational system is quite powerless to affect life adversely; it may be that any form of educational opportunity affords life the opportunity to select what it needs. No one knows enough to be dogmatic about it.

The most and the best Mr. Ford has sought to do in his educational program is to build according to his own best light.

34

Chapter III

THE NON-FAILURE SCHOOL

I

*T*HE "NON-FAILURE
School," as Mr. Ford explains it, means more
than non-failure in classrooms. What he is
aiming at is non-failure in life. He considers
the lowest grades the most important, since they
are the only grades attended by *all* the boys and
girls.

Right at the outset we are impressed by the
fact that the pupils in the lowest grades of the
Village schools propose much of their work
themselves. A six-year-old girl inquires about
the post-office. She has heard her parents
speak of it, and has learned that a mailman
brings letters to her home. Her natural curiosity leads her to ask, "What's a post-office?
How does the mail get into it?"

An inquiry of that sort is never left unanswered. First, the class is taken to the Village post-office and given a glimpse of its operations. Next day one of the older boys brings to class a crude mailbox he has nailed together, with a slot for letters at its top side. During one of the classes, envelopes are cut out and pasted together. Simple letters are written and placed in them. Another lesson covers the subject of stamps. At drawing-time stamps are made on the envelopes. The letters are deposited in the box and a mailman, chosen from their number, unlocks it and distributes the mail. Finally, pupils who are collecting stamps bring their albums for the others to see.

Another illustration might be found in the study of radio, usually regarded as slightly beyond the grasp of little minds. An older boy brings to school a microphone built by him at home. The children plan a broadcast. They rehearse carefully and on the appointed day, with an announcer they have selected, give the program into the homemade microphone, showing as much zest as they would have displayed in a regular studio.

To little ones in the lower grades, telling

38

time is always intriguing. "Teacher, how do you tell time?" asks a first-grade youngster in the McGuffey school. Out of the question grows a study of clocks. The lad who asked it obtains an empty coffee can at home and from it makes a clock dial. Something is missing; it needs hands. Why? What are the hands for? The entire class participates in the study and shortly all are surprising their parents by telling time at home.

"Learning by Doing" might be glimpsed in a project carried out by older boys and girls studying pioneer development. A 75-year-old log cabin in Greenfield Village became their laboratory. One committee drew floor plans. Another laid out the rooms on the floor of the museum and from the vast collection of Americana, selected furnishings that seemed appropriate to such a log cabin in the Mid-West a century ago. Each article was considered carefully, and discarded if not in keeping with the times and circumstances. After the instructor had finally approved their choice, the furnishings were set up in the cabin itself. Then the pupils met one evening at the cabin and ate a

39

dinner cooked on the old wood stove by the girls of the class.

II

When the first of the Edison Institute schools was opened in Greenfield Village on September 16, 1929, its student body comprised thirty-two pupils who had been chosen at random from the Dearborn Public Schools and brought in to form the nucleus. They commenced at the first grade and continued through the fourth, with four boys and four girls making up each—a quadrille set. The pupils of that fourth grade, after eight years of instruction here, gave the Institute the first class of seniors to graduate from its high school in June, 1937.

At this point it might be mentioned that ordinarily pupils do not enter the school except through the lowest grade or kindergarten. While exceptions can be made, Mr. Ford prefers that the child be trained from the outset. He feels that the experiment to prove its worth must take the pupil at the very beginning, and not after three, four, or eight years of study under a different system.

40

The youngsters who made up the first four classes were not picked because they were above the average in intelligence or pleasing personality. Rather, they were brought in from some of the city's overcrowded schools. Nor were they confined to children of Ford employes. As a goodly percentage of Dearborn homes are occupied by Ford employes, about an equal ratio of employes' children were included among the thirty-two, but no more. They did not come from the families of the topnotch executives. The son or daughter of a gate watchman or a farm foreman was included just as readily as the son or daughter of the advertising manager or the chief engineer.

From this group, the school has expanded slowly year by year, as each grade has advanced and a new first grade has enrolled to fill the gap at the bottom of the ladder. In the fall of 1937, the addition of a kindergarten made it, rather than the first grade, the source of recruits. Older pupils are brought in only when a vacancy exists, which is seldom.

On the opening day Mr. Ford appeared before the hand bell had rung, and shook hands

41

with each of the little ones. He sat with his old seatmate, Dr. Edsel A. Ruddiman, in the far corner they had occupied as boys, and each carved his initials on the desk top as they had more than half a century earlier in the days of the old Scotch Settlement near Dearborn. Mrs. Ford, Mr. and Mrs. Edsel Ford, and several of the latter's children were present. A young man who had been on the Trade School faculty was the first teacher. Later it was decided that a woman teacher should be used.

At the end of the first year the little brick school was overcrowded. Instead of thirty-two pupils, there were fifty-six. Instead of seeking recruits, the school was being flooded with requests from parents to admit their children. To provide more room, another building in the Village, the Town Hall, was assigned to the school's use, and equipped with desks. Another teacher was employed, and twenty-four pupils placed under her charge.

Expansion of the school continued. Classrooms in the Museum building, which up to now had remained idle, were prepared for

42

junior high school pupils, twenty-one of whom entered there in February, 1934.

In that same year Mr. Ford sent his representative into Washington County in Western Pennsylvania to obtain for him the old homestead where William Holmes McGuffey had been born. The tumble-down cabin was brought to the Village, restored and supplied with McGuffey furniture. Additional logs were hauled north and used in the framing of a school, named for McGuffey. In this new school the first and second grades were housed. The site of the old cabin was marked by Mr. Ford with an appropriate boulder and plaque, which he helped dedicate on the anniversary of McGuffey's birthday in September, 1934.

Meanwhile a high school faculty headed by Herman Grophear from the Dearborn school system was organized, to complete the upper grades in accordance with the "Learning by Doing" theory, and also to supply the required subjects to round out a high school education. A science laboratory, a music room, a library,— these and other equipment were added.

Sewing, weaving, choral singing, horseback

43

riding, athletic sports, housekeeping economics, manual training, pottery, machine shop, drafting, dancing—all these were taught under separate instructors.

A school paper was started under an experienced newspaperman. Instruction was given in organ playing, on the violin, and other instruments. An amateur radio station with complete apparatus was provided. Amateur photography was encouraged. Automobiles were torn down and assembled, and made available for those older ones who wished to learn how to drive, operate and repair a car. These and much more helped to round out the preparation of pupils for life.

III

Vacation time sees no cessation of the "outside" activities. Books and lessons are laid away, but teachers and pupils remain. Education is not a ten-month process in these schools; it goes on throughout the summer, with instructors working on a twelve-month basis. They have two weeks for a trip or recreation, and time

44

off for summer school should they choose to attend. Otherwise they occupy themselves with the pupils, who throng the Village campus even as they did while classes were in session.

Many recreational pursuits may be followed. Each morning the riding master leads out a platoon of girls or boys mounted on steeds from the Village stable for instruction in horsemanship. In the fresh-water lagoon below the Stephen Foster House—the Suwanee River—they splash, dive and swim, or, if they prefer, go boating and fishing under the watchful eye of an experienced swimmer. If they enjoy tennis, they may compete on the courts in a tournament arranged for them and umpired by a skilled tennis coach.

In these pastimes both boys and girls participate. Other occupations are restricted to one sex. For the girls, there is the sewing circle where materials are supplied for them to make any article desired, and a competent woman supervises their work with the needle. Others who weave may ply a loom in the Weave Shed, design patterns and make objects to be sold, enabling them to earn money.

45

Older girls from the high school who wish to earn money through office work are assigned to the stenographic department, to telephone switchboards, to filing and the various other lines serving the Ford industry, and are paid for their services. Still others do camera work, assist in Social Service, aid the teachers in caring for little children, and help edit the summer editions of the school paper.

The boys have equally wide variety of occupations. The pattern shop, machine shop, furniture repair shop, the farms, print shop—here may be found boys twelve years old and up earning their hourly wage and learning a useful trade. As already has been pointed out, learning how to earn is an important part of the Ford educational program. If a boy turns out a product that is not satisfactory he must do it over again and correct its faults in order to be paid for it. He is taught not to hurry his work, that quality is the first consideration. He is allowed to work only part time, at first, with afternoon hours free for tennis and swimming. As he becomes older he is trusted with more important tasks—driving test cars, work-

46

ing on the drafting-board, playing the chapel organ.

During vacation time also they must tend their gardens. These tracts are watched closely and a youngster who allows the weeds to over-run the rows of vegetables is not credited with the hours that go to the lad or lass whose tract is kept well cultivated. The families enjoy such produce as is needed, and the balance is sold by pupils at a roadside market. This money accumulates into a fund that is distrib-uted in the fall among all who have contributed toward it.

Thus school keeps on regardless of the fact that it is supposed to be "out." The signifi-cant thing about it is that the children them-selves flock back to the scenes of their studies after they have been released to go elsewhere. They don't want to leave school. This, accord-ing to Mr. Ford's ideas, is more natural. If education is in truth a part of life itself, why should it end arbitrarily every summer for two or three months? Life does not break off that way, and there would be less distinction be-

47

tween education and life if the former process were made as continuing as the latter.

IV

Near the end of the Village devoted to early American homes stands a white colonial residence of the early eighteenth century that once graced the summit of a hill at Exeter, New Hampshire. Because it was formerly occupied by a Secretary of State for that commonwealth, it bears the name "Secretary House." It has been set aside for a clubhouse for girls of the upper grades in the Edison Institute.

In regular rotation they spend nights or week-ends here, learning housekeeping and the arts of homemaking by "doing." Those who are to act as hostesses arrive at the house as soon as classes are finished for the day, and under the general supervision of a resident-mistress, plan the evening dinner menu. They are then taken to the market to shop and return to prepare and cook the food, set the table and get ready for other girls who are to be guests.

After dinner, dishes are washed, wiped and

48

● Looking past the porch of Stephen Foster House toward the McGuffey log cabin birthplace, Greenfield Village.

● Secretary House from New Hampshire, used as a clubhouse by girl students of Edison Institute.

put away, and the crumbs swept, after which the girls are free for evening pursuits. In addition to a large library of phonograph records for music, there are radio amplifiers in each room, operated from a central control board. On social evenings some of the young men may drop in to dance in the recreation room. Or on summer days, a jelly-making bee may occupy the girls.

In the morning, breakfast is cooked, beds are made and the house placed in order before the girls leave for home or school.

While the furnishings of this fine old mansion are all authentic pieces of classical style from the Museum, no attempt has been made to supply all of them in any one room from the same period. By having a Duncan Phyfe table in the same room as a William-and-Mary highboy, it is thought that the pupil will discern distinguishing characteristics more readily than if both pieces were Phyfe.

Nor are all appliances of the most modern sort. While it is true that the house possesses the most modern gas and electric ranges, it also has coal and wood ranges, as well as an old-time

49

fireplace, with which the girls are taught to cook. A young girl never knows in advance the circumstances of the man whom she is to marry, Mr. Ford believes; and there may be some in the school who will find knowledge of coal or wood stoves helpful when they start homes of their own.

There are many features of this old clubhouse to make it attractive to the pupils. Behind the staircase along the chimney is a secret door that opens into a concealed chamber, with hidden steps ascending to the upstairs and attic. A lovely garden filled with all varieties of old-fashioned flowers, an upper porch looking down on the athletic field, shelves filled with interesting books—these are a few of the enticements that distinguish it from a home economics laboratory devoted solely to instruction.

v

Mention has been made of the weekly morning broadcasts over a national network. In line with the plan to Learn by Doing, the children of the schools carry out the broadcasts

50

themselves. One student presides at the chapel organ, another acts as announcer at the microphone, and still others contribute solos or recitations as called upon. There is nothing about the process to make them self-conscious; indeed, the poise of the littlest ones before the "mike" would do credit to the most experienced performers. This is partly true because of the natural manner in which they become familiar with it; they literally grow up with it.

Performing on the stage before a packed audience is another experience with which they grow up. In the operettas and other school programs, the wee ones have simple acts that include costumes and scenery. Their theater is perfectly equipped. It forms the auditorium of the Museum and has border lights, drops and dressing-rooms. By the time the first-graders have reached high school age they are as much at ease before the footlights as behind the "mike."

Some have remarked on the multitude of extra-curricular activities that mark the training of these pupils. These are designed to leave little or no idle time for the students.

51

They are kept busier than perhaps any children of their age anywhere. A trip to see a World's Series game or a World's Fair, to help a threshing crew or cook a threshing dinner, to see a Gilbert and Sullivan opera or attend a symphony concert—anything is considered valuable as a part of the classroom work.

Two characteristics have been noted in the pupils—first, that they are mentally alert: their minds are awake. They are more than mystified lookers-on at life: they are intelligent participants in all that goes on. Second, that they are open and frank in their approach and inquiries. They have been taught that it is their duty and right to *know*, and they exercise it.

VI

In all these activities, Mr. Ford is not only the director and inspirer, but also an active participant. He has been, in fact, since the schools were opened in 1929. During the school year he invariably attends the early morning chapel service unless he is absent from Dearborn, and when he is away, he tunes in on

52

the weekly broadcast. They know he is listening with Mrs. Ford, for not infrequently telegrams are received from him regarding some feature of the program.

After the buses have unloaded the pupils behind Clinton Inn at the edge of the Village green, and the company of young folks wends its way to the Chapel at the green's head, Mr. Ford appears and joins them. Sometimes he is accompanied by Mrs. Ford, sometimes by a personal friend, sometimes by one of the children. Occasionally he invites a guest to meet him here and join him in listening to the service. The children treat him as one of themselves, thronging about him at times. During the service he sits in the choir loft, and it is a rule of the assembly below in the pews not to turn and stare at him. They respect his presence and have no wish to embarrass him.

Frequently he suggests innovations for their program. It was he who proposed old tunes of his youth for verses from the McGuffey Readers that he had memorized as a boy and still recalls. The children learned the tunes and occasionally sing them for him. Old favorites

53

of his, such as "I Love to Tell the Story," and
his friend Edison's songs, such as "I'll Take
You Home Again, Kathleen," are often part
of the program. On special days—the birth-
days of men like Stephen Foster, Dr. McGuffey,
Lincoln, Edison, and Washington—the entire
program is commemorative of the man.

The chapel service is only one part of his
interest in the schools. In the early evening
his car may drive to the gardens, and pupils
hoeing weeds may be joined by him. Often
he chats with them till dusk falls. With every
activity he is in intimate and constant touch.
Rehearsals of school operettas or plays find
him seated in the back of the theater, listening.
Noonday luncheon at the Clinton Inn may
find him dropping in. More often than not
he visits the Secretary House to spend a treas-
ured half-hour with the girl students, or perhaps eat supper with them. Shop, farm, camp
—wherever they are he is sure to take an interest. And on each scholar's birthday, a personal
telegram from him arrives with a lovely cake
as surely as the day itself.

54

Chapter IV

SCHOOLS OF THE INSTITUTE

I

*A*LREADY IT HAS
been stated that the ideas to which Mr. Ford
is giving realization did not come of sudden
birth, but had been in his mind for years waiting for the time to become ripe when they could
be put into effect. More than twenty years ago
he was planning them, along with his great collection of Americana, and the decentralization
of industry into rural plants.

In the spring of 1919 he was interviewed by
a reporter for the monthly magazine *Reconstruction,* in the course of which the reporter's
wife asked him:

"You speak of education, Mr. Ford. What
is your idea of education? What would you
want to teach?"

"I should say that the purpose of education

is to make people do what they don't want to do."

"Do you really mean that?"

"Yes, of course; they'll do what they want to do without being educated."

He added: "I am going to tell the young men to find useful things to do, because that is the way to be happy in this world. There is no other way to happiness, and the man who seeks it any other way is going astray. If you work and work hard and work faithfully, success is certain to you. . . . That is the one great message I want to give to young men."

When he visited Edison at West Orange in 1927 on the occasion of the inventor's eightieth birthday anniversary, he was quoted by the newspaper reporters as saying:

"I think education is the greatest force in civilization and the most deserving of help."

The statement was made in response to suggestions as to how he could spend his money, and gave basis to the rumor that he proposed to devote it to education.

Now that he is taking time to apply his educational ideas, he fully expects to see them

58

carried through to a point where professional pedagogues may appraise them for definite results. He himself, of course, makes no pretense to being anything but a mechanical engineer by profession, but he believes that engineering and industry can contribute important new truths to education—and should.

Another purpose of education as he views it was expressed by him when he said, "Life is a going concern. It is going somewhere. It never stagnates. That is one reason I like to watch and talk with the youngsters at the schools in Greenfield Village.

"What I greatly hope for these children, and for children everywhere, is a new attitude toward life—free from the gullibility which thinks we can get something for nothing; free from the greed which thinks any permanent good can come of overreaching others: and, above all, expectant of change, so that when life gives them a jolt they will be fully prepared to push on eagerly along new lines."

This was reiterated by Mr. W. J. Cameron in addressing the first graduating class from the high school in June, 1937:

59

"The other motive behind the educational idea operating here is to make you forever immune to the fallacies that deceive and dislocate so many uninformed or misinformed people today. Racketeers not only seek to purloin your money, there are racketeers that seek to purloin your mind also. Your school desires to get you beyond the possibilities of being victimized by either of these snares. . . . Your school wants you to be in control of your mentality and your material affairs. It wants you to be the beginning of a race of Americans that will offer no soil for the seeds of deception."

II

It would be impractical to allow the many visitors who throng Greenfield Village and the Museum to view the schools in operation, for no pupils could be expected to concentrate on study when under the gaze of several thousand strangers daily. Those who because of their profession have a special interest in education are sometimes granted permits to inspect classes, but these are necessarily restricted.

60

Parents of pupils, of course, are free to visit classes at any time.

During the summer vacation the brick Scotch Settlement School is thrown open to visitors and is inspected daily by them. The remaining buildings used by the system—the Ann Arbor House, the log McGuffey School, the Town Hall School and the Secretary House— remain on the closed list, being reserved for the use of the pupils and teachers in their vacation activities. Many questions are asked as to the interior construction and equipment of these buildings, and about the School system in general.

First, in order of instruction at least, is the kindergarten, occupying the lovely Ann Arbor House, a white residence on the shaded lane not far from the girls' clubhouse.

In this building the first pre-school class to join the Village system gathered in September, 1937, with sixteen pupils, eight boys and eight girls enrolled.

Upon arriving in the morning the children pass through a center hall into one of the adjoining rooms, where they find closets with

61

coathooks well within their reach. The front room on the right serves as a sort of reception-room. Gaily colored wallpaper presents small pictures of children at play in the various seasons, interspersed with familiar seasonal references: "The North Wind doth blow," "The Bullfrog in the Pool," and so on. An easel and a small blackboard are part of this room's equipment.

Through a wide archway it is but a step into the library where an old-fashioned fireplace takes up one end of a room, studded with low-shelved bookcases filled with attractive children's books.

Differing from the usual procedure for young children, the pupils have sessions morning and afternoon instead of half a day. Luncheon is served at noon in the room at the left of the center hall. Low round tables, each with four small chairs, are here. Scenes and sayings from Mother Goose Rhymes form the wallpaper pattern. Good conduct is stressed as in all the other school dining-halls, and after the meal the little ones take turns drying the dishes.

Recreational facilities such as blocks, bal-

62

ance beams, and a piano are in the basement. This has been furnished in a light airy mode in keeping with the rest of the building, and the sharp corners have been rounded off so the children may have a safe place to play. The same is true of the edges of the low stone wall bordering steps leading from the back porch to the service drive in the rear. The large veranda provides a cool and refreshing spot for incidental activities on hot afternoons.

When time for their rest period arrives, the boys and girls go upstairs to separate rooms where they may nap on comfortable cots.

Instruction is of the usual type, except that children are taught to use their hands whenever possible. Dancing lessons, rides in pony carriages, nature trips, and health exercises comprise part of each day's program.

The primary McGuffey school, though built of logs, is ultra-modern in its lighting and heating. Artificial illumination is indirect along the upper edges of the walls just below the ceiling. Air-conditioned throughout, the building is snugly comfortable in winter and

63

cool in summer. No open chinks admit the January blasts, for the interior is paneled.

The furnishings are old and new. For example, the teacher's desk was once used by Dr. McGuffey himself. A fireplace with mantel fills the far end of the room. On the wall are illustrations reproduced from the McGuffey Readers. Supplies are kept in a McGuffey corner cupboard.

Individual desks of the pupils are light, strong and designed to accommodate the small bodies in comfort. Those of the smallest tots are lower, permitting their feet to rest on the floor. The combination desk-chair is shaped something like the traditional cafeteria chair with a book compartment suspended below the flat arm-rest. The latter opens, serving as the lid of the compartment.

Inasmuch as it is difficult for the little hands to extract pencils, pens or erasers from among these books, a separate sliding drawer has been concealed beneath the chair seat, where it can be drawn out easily.

A notable feature of the school is the basement. Adapted to recreation use during win-

64

ter recesses, it also serves as a supplemental classroom. In one corner, pupils form a circle of small chairs to watch slides projected on the screen from a lantern.

Filling the center of the room is a low table built to hold typewriters at a convenient angle. Nearby are small looms specially designed to teach the first and second graders the first principles of weaving. These looms have no treadles, both of the operations being made by hand.

About the basement are evidences of careful planning. Projecting corners and supporting pillars are padded with leather to protect little heads from hard bumps. The washstand and towel rack are low enough for the tiniest arms and hands to reach.

How Mr. Ford's interest in the McGuffey Readers chanced to be re-awakened many years ago was related by Mr. W. J. Cameron in one of his talks on the Ford Sunday Evening Hour. A group of school-children happened to race past the house where he and Mrs. Ford were at the time. She quoted:

65

"Hear the children gaily shout,
  'Half-past four and school is out!' "

She remarked, "I wonder what the rest of the piece was."

Both recalled it as an excerpt from one of the McGuffey Readers, and a search was made among her old school-books. The First Reader could not be located. They instituted a search among their friends—sought the old bookshops —and were rewarded with a number of First Readers.

Mr. Ford commenced reprinting the six Eclectic Readers about 1926, since which time he has given away more than 5,000 to schools, colleges and to libraries, to statesmen and educators, and to many average citizens.

Among the trees and shrubbery bordering the McGuffey group in the Village are two tiny buildings that form a part of the primary school equipment although they have no connection with Dr. McGuffey. A playhouse and a barn—diminutive in size—they form a unique laboratory for introducing the first and second graders to life. The house has two rooms, each completely furnished. A grown person must

66

stoop to enter the doorway or else bump his head. Chairs, table, cook stove, drain sink, and other furnishings are the proper size for little ones. The latter helped prepare many of the furnishings, such as the window curtains. The little barn shelters two Shetland ponies and a miniature wagon for their use and care.

III

On attaining the third grade, pupils leave the log school and move to the Scotch Settlement or Town Hall School.

While the interior of the former building has been restored to resemble as closely as possible that known to the youthful Henry Ford when he attended here, at the same time conveniences have been modernized. A large wood stove fills the space fronting the teacher's desk; its pipe stretches overhead entirely across the room to the far wall. But the heating is actually done by a modern furnace in the basement. The blackboards are still wooden, but modern air-conditioning keeps the room at an even temperature. Outlets for heat are con-

67

cealed along the edge of the rostrum. Coal-oil
lamps stand in wonted brackets along the wall,
but the pupils are not compelled to strain their
eyes by kerosene light. Artificial illumination
is by electricity, the lights being hidden from
view behind the moldings.

Each of the old-style double desks provides
seating and book space for two pupils sitting
side by side. These pupils, like those in the
Town Hall School and the high school, are
served a hot lunch each noon in the dining-
room of Clinton Inn, a century-old tavern that
has been restored in the Village. Fresh milk
is served to all pupils during the middle of both
morning and afternoon periods.

After a pupil has graduated from the seventh
grade he leaves the Village school for classes in
the Museum building, where two floors of one
section have been set aside for their use. In
addition to the usual courses common to most
high schools, they are able to pursue special
studies in the Museum itself as well as elsewhere. Many outside trips are made, to the
Rouge plant of the Ford Motor Company with
the science teacher, to a nearby bank with a

68

mathematics instructor, to an opera with the music teacher, to a major league baseball game with the coach. The radio students have visited all the important stations in the surrounding territory. Longer trips have included tours to the Chicago World's Fair, to the Ways, Georgia, region where the boy students helped dismantle a rice-mill, and many others. Students have occupied their summers in varied ways. Several high school girls have gone to Europe. One of the older boys was chosen to accompany an exploring expedition in the West. Four boys operated a farm.

Use of these facilities by the high school pupils required the development of a new technique in instruction methods. It would be fatal, of course, to permit youngsters of junior high school age to roam without adequate preparation among the unique and often valuable, almost priceless objects Mr. Ford has assembled. Before they are ready to study the collections and investigate the $8\frac{1}{2}$ acres of exhibition hall, they must be made familiar with the physical layout, so as not to get lost; and must be given definite projects or objectives.

69

One method that proved successful among the seventh and eighth graders was a scavenger hunt. Hints or clues were given them pointing to thirty-five objects easily accessible, names of cars or airplanes, numbers on locomotives, and so on. While the pupils were locating these, they were learning many other things that awakened their interest in the collections.

Then came a second, more difficult "hunt" confined to the Agricultural and Textile sections, and occupying six periods on three different days. Fifty-three articles were listed, one point counting for each. The students hunted in pairs. Some of the puzzling references were "2A," "Wheeler and Wilson," "L. Boles, His Bottle," "Whittemore's." Others, such as the John Deere plow, were not hard to locate. The leaders had found forty-one of the fifty-three when time was called.

Development of this technique has progressed since the classes moved into the building. It is not surprising to learn that the older pupils have come to appreciate the treasures, handle them properly, and conduct research in a careful and accurate manner.

70

IV

A significant addition to the Edison Institute came with the opening of a technical institute, offering advanced courses in mechanical, electrical, chemical and agricultural engineering. To house this important addition to the curriculum, a new large building of red brick and marble was constructed east of the Museum during 1937.

In size it is, roughly, 300 feet by 300 feet, though its form is not square. It has central buildings and four wide wings, front and rear. Within are two interior courts with planting areas and flagstone walks. On every side but the north, whose principal unit is the natatorium, are porches and terraces—eight in all, and second-story terraces overlooking the inner courts.

Though in architectural harmony with its neighbors, the building was given a somewhat more delicate style than the Museum, with whose sturdy Doric columns the 28-foot shafts of the Corinthian-capped columns of its two-story porch on the south façade contrast pleas-

71

antly. It is a pure type of American Colonial architecture, strongly reminiscent of many fine old buildings frequently encountered in Virginia and Maryland.

Entrance to the building is through a spacious lobby on the Museum side. A technical library opens off the lobby on the left, while on the opposite side a grand staircase winds up to the second-floor ballroom, one of the loveliest of its kind.

White-walled, it is fronted by a reception lounge with retiring-rooms on either hand. Mulberry-colored heavy damask draperies frame the high windows. Entrance to the floor is through wide arched openings that permit an uninterrupted view from the top of the staircase to the far side. The floor is of polished teakwood, and the three overhead crystal chandeliers are of exquisite design. At the eastern side is the shell with its stage where the old-time orchestra sits. Seats for the dancers line the walls. When this ballroom was formally opened on the evening of October 26, 1937, Mr. Edsel Ford announced that it had been named "Lovett Hall" in honor of Mr. and Mrs.

72

B. B. Lovett, who for thirteen years have been in charge of the old-time dancing instruction.

The first class of technical students reported September 18, 1937, with thirty-six high school graduates, twenty-nine young men and seven young women. The morning program was given over to classes, while the afternoons were spent in gaining actual experience in work associated with the course selected. A lad interested in agricultural engineering might work at canning tomatoes, one of mechanical bent might take an automobile engine apart. Mr. O. C. Hood, principal of the Dearborn high school, was selected by the Institute to direct their work.

The various laboratories in the building have been equipped with the most modern scientific apparatus. Each of the students receives a regular weekly scholarship in the form of money earned while in school.

v

In this building, also, is a complete gymnasium and physical education department for all

73

the pupils in the Institute schools. Coaches for both boys and girls comprise the athletic faculty. A swimming-pool has been placed in the building for their use, with water from two to nine feet deep resting in highly colored ceramic tile illuminated by submarine lights.

Physical health is considered as essential as mental and moral in the Ford schools, and a complete athletic schedule is maintained ranging from pupils in the kindergarten with their exercises to competitive teams in the upper grades.

In addition, a doctor and nurse from the Henry Ford Hospital are present at the beginning of school each morning to check minor ailments and advise treatment when necessary. The health of the pupils is guarded assiduously, and more than one child who has required an operation or hospitalization has received it.

Dance training, both in the old-fashioned and modern steps, is not confined to the Institute schools. Several years ago Mr. Ford consented to lend his instructor to a few Dearborn schools who had requested it. He also arranged for classes from the schools to use his ballroom,

74

in the afternoon for younger ones and in the early evening for the older. At the disposal of these classes has been his old-time orchestra. To climax the work, an annual contest for dance-callers was arranged, the winner to receive a trophy from Mr. Ford.

As the years went on, more and more Dearborn schools were added to the list, and then schools of metropolitan Detroit requested instruction. To accommodate them, a staff of selected young men was trained under his direction and supplied wherever needed at no expense to the school. During the summer of 1937 a second class was organized among guides of Greenfield Village, and a third among young men outside the Village.

Instruction in the old-time dances among school-children in that area has been spreading rapidly, as a result.

It is Mr. Ford's hope that the important education resources of Village and Museum will be made available to classes and pupils of schools everywhere. For several years teachers have been permitted to bring their scholars by bus to Dearborn to view the project and receive the inspiration it invariably gives to young people.

Recently inquiries were made as to the possibility of bringing an entire student body from a nearby city to spend all day at the Edison Institute. This could be done only if special trainloads could be given parking space on the Village siding. Mr. Ford gladly assisted in this, and during 1936 as many as 2,500 pupils, comprising three special trains of twenty coaches each, drew in on the track in a single day. On another occasion, all the schools in an entire county were closed to enable their pupils to make the trip. On warm spring days, senior classes from twenty or more different high schools roam the grounds on the same afternoon.

Out of this came a request from Wayne University to inaugurate a course in which schoolteachers themselves could learn about Museum and Village, and thus be able more intelligently to prepare their pupils in advance of the visit, with a better comprehension of what was in store.

A graduate course was added to the university's College of Education, wherein graduate

76

credits could be earned by teachers enrolling in it. The course proved so popular that an advanced one was added, offering opportunity for research among selected subjects dealing with the project. Finally, a summer school course was arranged with six weeks of classes during the 1937 vacation. Members of Village and Museum staff acted as instructors.

Chapter V

RURAL SCHOOLS

I

*T*HE TEACHING
methods and McGuffey ideals that have char-
acterized the schools of the Edison Institute at
Dearborn are by no means restricted to them.
Wherever Mr. Ford has gone in the past ten
years or so—among the northern pines on the
cool shores of Lake Superior in midsummer,
among the giant water oaks of sunny Georgia
in midwinter, in rural districts of his own Michigan, even across the ocean in England—the
seed of his ideas have sprung into flowering.

Within a radius of one hundred miles from
his home, he has acquired since 1927 many
hundreds of acres of farmlands to use in experimenting with the soybean. Lying chiefly
in Lenawee and Washtenaw Counties, these
back country districts have awakened into new

81

activity. Old homes have been restored, schools have reopened, dam sites have been rebuilt, mills have resumed operations as part of his village industries, and parks and man-made lakes have beautified the countryside. Forgotten towns have been resurrected from half a century of sleep into new life.

Where winding gravel roads leave the paved highways and thread among the broad acres of farm and woodland, six district schools have been reinstated. They are one-room schools with the teacher instructing in all the grades just as he did three-quarters of a century ago. But the textbooks and equipment are most modern, and in addition many other courses are taught by special visiting instructors. An even more important adjunct is the opportunity to participate in many of the activities of the Edison Institute, including sojourns at the Secretary House.

Five of the schools are situated in the region west and south of Dearborn within an hour's drive. The Stone Pennington School is oldest in years, the date of its erection being 1851. It bears the name of a pioneer Quaker settler

82

who migrated to the Raisin River valley early in the nineteenth century and built a log cabin on the banks of a nearby creek. As others joined him the spot became known as Pennington's Corners. In time a log school was built to minister to the needs of the children, later being supplanted by one of stone.

As years went by the settlement—then known as Macon—dwindled to an almost neglected hamlet of a few families. The run-down houses preserved but a shadow of their former beauty. When in 1931 Mr. Ford found the village in the heart of the lands he had acquired for soybean experiments, he restored not only the stone school (which was being used as a warehouse in the rear of a store), but also two of the lovely white houses that had graced this countryside half a century previously. On the day the school was reopened, nineteen of the thirty-one living members of its first classes sat in their old places and answered roll-call.

The interior was restored in the original black walnut. School desks were made of large-growth timber, glue joints not being needed for seats, seat backs, ends or lids; and were so ar-

83

ranged as to face stove and teacher's platform from three directions.

Some distance east of Macon near the edge of the soybean acres Mr. Ford found a red brick country school with windows shuttered and door locked. It had been erected shortly before the outbreak of the Civil War to replace a frame structure on the banks of the Willow Run Creek. It had a beautiful white ash floor, long, comfortable and individual desks. To it for his first teaching assignment in 1888 came Frank Cody, in later years Detroit's distinguished superintendent of schools and president of Wayne University.

In the same month that saw the reopening of the Stone Pennington School, classes met once more at the Willow Run School. A little band of oldtimers were present to celebrate the occasion, and Dr. Cody came to ring the old hand bell and call them to order.

Distinctive as were these two rural schools, their charm was surpassed by a third that he restored—the Green Lane Academy. This small brick edifice stood at the end of an evergreen-bordered lane not far from the vil-

84

lage of Tecumseh, where it was built in 1869 to provide additional facilities for that neighborhood. It stood on a sloping bank and had two stories. Later it was diverted to use as a dwelling, continuing as such till Mr. Ford purchased it early in 1932 for restoration as a kindergarten.

Instruction of the pre-school children in this rural neighborhood is interesting and varied. A description of an average days' program as prepared for *The Herald*—told of the activities as follows:

A DAY AT GREEN LANE ACADEMY

It is nine o'clock and the little old-fashioned bell sends out its notes calling the children into the little red schoolhouse to start a day's work.

First comes the daily health inspection at which time the children are examined for any signs of illness or disease. The next fifteen or twenty minutes are spent in singing, after which the children repeat the Lord's Prayer and the Twenty-third Psalm in unison. They now listen to stories or, on some days, they alternate and they dramatize the stories they have heard. The remainder of the time before the morning recess is spent in printing and learning the alphabet.

After a very lively and much enjoyed recess, each

85

child comes into the schoolhouse for a glass of tomato-juice and a few minutes' rest. They then have their little orchestra practice, after which they are taught words, with lantern slides.

The noon hour has arrived, and the little tots go trooping downstairs for their lunches, which are prepared for them by one of the teachers.

At one o'clock the notes of the little bell again ring forth, and the children, now divided into two groups, settle themselves for another rest. After the rest period a few minutes are spent in number work, and during the remaining time before dismissal the youngsters busy themselves by drawing pictures and coloring in their color books.

II

At the opening of the Stone Pennington School, Mr. W. J. Cameron in his address explained something of Mr. Ford's object. He said:

"The district school keeps education close to the home and farm. In those district school days, we were the board of education. We levied the taxes, we hired the teachers, and we furnished the wood. There was time for contacts, stimulation of the social emotions and the cultivation of character. The effect of

86

community influences was felt in the school-room; it is a remote thing in modern educational systems.

"This experiment by Mr. Ford is an attempt to see if there is a service which the district school can perform in this generation. It is to be an example on a modest scale of what America possessed educationally when she raised her greatest men."

Three district schools for which he is "good angel" have not yet been described. One was built in 1876 and in honor of that year was called the "Centennial" School. It stands about three miles south and east of Tecumseh, and like the Green Lane Academy is built of brick. On the fall day in 1932 when it was reopened, a silver-haired woman who had taught it a generation ago, called the pupils to their classes.

In the town of Tecumseh is the Brownville brick school in which, as in the Stone Pennington and Centennial Schools, grades from one through twelve are taught. It was named for one of the first settlers of this region, General Jacob Brown, and was known in the 8o's as the North Branch School. After having been

87

abandoned for many years, it was reopened by Mr. Ford in 1933, completely restored with oil-lamps, box stove, and whitewood desks as in the earlier times.

Newest of the rural schools restored by Mr. Ford is that at Nankin Mills, a quiet corner among the maples where the Ann Arbor Trail crosses the Rouge River. Here is a century-old grist-mill restored by him some years ago and now used in producing dies and engravings for production. The red brick school was opened in the fall of 1937 to provide instruction for the youngsters of nearby farmers, many of whom find part-time employment in the restored mill.

In addition to these six schools there are others in the same areas that receive many benefits from him, participating in old-time dancing classes, gardens and other activities.

A few miles south of Willow Run School on the banks of the Huron River, a thriving settlement sprang up about a century ago around the log cabin of Ameriah Rawson. In time it became known as "Michigan City." In 1860 a new brick school was erected here, only to wit-

88

ness the slow demise of the "City" as mills and shops moved away. The name was changed to Rawsonville, but that was not sufficient to keep interest alive. A few scattered houses, a deserted tavern and a slowly dying school greeted Mr. Ford when he drove into the valley. Under his encouragement it has found new life.

Also dating back to 1860 is the Mills School near Macon settlement, a frame structure on the site of the first school in Lenawee County. It was named for Gabriel Mills, an early settler who built a dam on Macon Creek and cut logs in a sawmill. His son, Cassius Mills, at the age of 84, looked down from the ancestral home a few years ago and with deep interest watched Mr. Ford restore the old dam and reconstruct the sawmill.

Another school is the Macon Town School which was added to the village in 1866 to accommodate an overflow of pupils from the Stone Pennington School. It was much more modern than the other, having desks with iron framework, and a bell in the cupola in the roof. Increasing population compelled the addition of a second room and employment of a second

89

teacher. High school subjects were then taught. Later as the growth stopped, and the town went into a decline, the addition was used as a storeroom till Mr. Ford remodeled the building in 1931 and arranged for its reopening.

Two other district schools in the vicinity of Tecumseh to be aided by him are the Waring, west of the Centennial, and the Comfort, not far from Green Lane Academy. The former was opened in the fall of 1934 after it had been closed a few years. The latter was built in 1872 on the Comfort farm, of brick supplied by Elwood Comfort.

III

In all the schools—both those entirely directed by the Institute and those supplied with books and equipment—agriculture is a part of the curriculum. No youngster is too small to learn about nature, growing plants or the value of the soil. This applies to city as well as country. At the Wayside Inn Boy's School in South Sudbury, Massachusetts, he has instituted a four-year agricultural course.

90

When the Boys School was opened by Mr. Ford in March, 1928, thirty boys formed the nucleus of the student body. At first the courses emphasized the development of character and preparation for future careers. In 1933 the curriculum was broadened to include a four-year agricultural program. The enrolment increased to forty-four day and boarding scholars, a headmaster, two teachers of agricultural and two for academic subjects.

The activities of these boys are in line with the ideas of the founder, and just as varied as those at the Edison Institute. Projects in agriculture predominate, of course, from poultry raising to greenhouse culture, the boys providing not only the actual care but also constructing the necessary equipment, even the buildings. They have the usual athletic teams and contests. They also have a two weeks' recreational camp in midsummer. Occasionally they are taken on informative trips resembling those of the Edison Institute older pupils. Before graduating, each senior class plants a tree on the grounds, using the Judge Shute spade.

91

Two buildings serve as dormitories. One of these, Dutton Lodge, is the largest structure on the grounds next to Wayside Inn itself, with two stories, cellar and attic. On the second floor are the students' and instructors' rooms. The ground floor houses the kitchen, dining-room, living-room, radio-room, and visitors' parlor, while in the cellar are the laundry-room, shower, locker and recreation-rooms. The other building is the Calvin How, situated on the old Boston Post Road, a historic structure that still carries the original dark red color once so popular in this region.

The procedure here may be understood better, perhaps, by a description of an ordinary day's program at the school prepared for the *Edison Institute Herald* by one of the pupils, Christopher Ganos:

A DAY AT DUTTON LODGE

At a quarter to six each morning, with the exception of Sunday, the boys are aroused from their sleep by the buzzer. The squad leader in charge goes around to each room to drag overzealous sleepers out of bed. A scuffle of slippered feet can be heard as the boys go down to take their showers. When they finish dress-

92

ing and make their beds they begin to tidy their respective rooms.

At a quarter to seven the buzzer sounds again. This
means inspection. The squad leader and the instructor
in charge go into each room and run their fingers over
the most unthought of places to find dust. If the instructor finds some he politely tells the boy to clean
the room more thoroughly or he will receive a penalty.

The boys from Calvin How come over to Dutton
about seven o'clock. The welcoming "clang" of the
bell is heard and all the boys go into the dining-room.
The metallic sound of spoons striking cereal bowls
issues from the dining-room. At 7:45 the buzzer again
sounds. This time it is assembly. Mr. Young, the
headmaster, reads from the Bible; after saying the
Lord's Prayer the boys hear the announcements for
the day.

After assembly is over the freshmen and seniors go
to class, and the sophomores and juniors to work.
With dinner over the sophomores and juniors go to
school, and the freshmen and seniors go to work. Our
daily schedule is so well planned that there is seldom
a mishap.

At five o'clock the boys go to their respective houses
and change their clothes for supper. After eating,
they go swimming, fishing, or doing whatever they desire. The dust has no time to collect on the pool-
table, because it is in constant use. At a quarter to
nine the boys go down to take showers and get ready
for bed. At nine o'clock it's "light out" for freshmen

93

and sophomores. At a quarter of ten all lights in the house go out.

Of the three schools comprising the Wayside Inn group, possibly the most interesting is the Redstone or Mary Lamb School. Certainly it is the oldest of all those under the Ford direction, for the original primitive temple of education was built about 1798, and continued in use until 1856. It was an ordinary wooden building painted red, with little benches for the very young and rude writing desks, and it stood on a rising called Redstone Hill, whence its name.

When Rebecca (Polly) Kimball taught the school, among her pupils was little Mary Elizabeth Sawyer, whose pet was a playful lamb. On the fateful morning that John Roulstone, nephew to the minister, visited school, the lamb followed Mary to school and the teacher turned it out because it made the children laugh and play. Roulstone's three verses, and those added later by Sarah Josepha Hale, were read by the youthful Henry Ford in McGuffey's old Second Reader.

The building was found in Sterling by Mr.

and Mrs. Ford and brought to the Wayside Inn grounds where it was restored and reopened as a school in January, 1927. Double wooden desks, large heater and long stovepipe extending across the length of the room were among its furnishings.

The foundations of the Southwest School are nearly as old as the Mary Lamb, for they are the original ones of a school which was constructed about 1800 in Sudbury. Some years after the superstructure had been destroyed by fire, the foundations were located by the position of four poplar trees, and upon it there was erected the present building. Twenty-three pupils of the fifth grades comprised the first student body to attend when it was reopened in the fall of 1930.

IV

What of the older girls in the Institute rural schools? For them, a School of Home Arts has been established in the heart of Detroit on the grounds of the Henry Ford Hospital. Its purpose is to furnish instruction in the arts of scientific home making and living.

95

The School was started for girl graduates of the schools located in Tecumseh, Macon, and similar places, and was intended to provide knowledge from experience gained during a year's stay at the Hospital, which could be applied in the home. Here the sciences and other subjects are taught in a way that will prepare the girls better to understand their daily tasks. For example, chemistry teaches them why they use baking-powder in cakes, biology why it is a good idea to disinfect wounds, and why it is best to use pasteurized milk.

Besides studying and going to classes, the girls run their own house in the Clara Ford Nurses' Home. Each one must learn to plan menus for the group, buy according to a fixed budget, cook well-balanced meals, and serve them attractively. They learn to sew and make dresses for themselves and some of the patients. Child care and training have been among their subjects, and each has two babies to care for, one over a year old and another just a few months old.

These girls have an interesting social life, with opportunities to attend concerts, the Ford

96

● Entrance Lobby, Recreation Building. Home of the new
technical school—Edison Institute.

● Waterford general store at edge of Village green, adjoining Clinton Inn.

Sunday Evening Hours, lectures at the Detroit
Institute of Arts, and many other cultural activities. The Nurses' Home gives informal
entertainments, and entertains many guests
during the year.

Their surroundings are attractive and healthful. Each girl has an individual bedroom with
desk, bed, lounge chair, and two tables. Among
the rooms are guest-rooms where the girls en-
tertain, a spacious living-room, a library for
study, a dining-room, and several sewing-rooms.

Healthful living is emphasized throughout
the year's instruction. The young ladies have
gymnasium classes to correct posture, and to
learn and enjoy sports. There is an attractive
swimming-pool which all enjoy. Good health
rules are learned and practised by these young
women, who some day it is expected will build
happy American homes.

v

During the cold months of dead winter, it is
the usual custom for those Northerners able to
retreat to the warmer climate in the Southland

97

to bask on the golden sands of the beaches, enjoy the thrill of deep-sea fishing, and generally to relax in a vacation mood. Edison, too, spent his winters near balmy Ft. Myers, but neither he nor his next-door neighbor, Mr. Ford, would ever be content to spend an idle vacation. Edison had a small laboratory wherein he could carry on such experiments as he chose, and where eventually he sought to produce rubber from the goldenrod.

After the inventor's death, Mr. Ford's attention centered more and more in the fertile Georgia country where considerable acreage was not being utilized, and there he began planning to continue his educational experiments, even while sojourning on a so-called winter "vacation" from the rigors of the Dearborn February.

The property acquired by him bordered the broad Ogeechee River west of Savannah in the eastern corner of the state, where South Carolina drops swiftly toward the ocean. A new condition confronted him here, in that many of the recipients of his educational ideas and benefits were to be Negroes.

98

About the year 1930 he began remodeling the dilapidated Cherry Hill School, and furnishing it with necessary fixtures for instruction. Soon he was adding other schools to his list—Oak Level, Port Royal, Park Hill, Strathy Hall and Fancy Hall.

An interesting description of what took place, contrasting prior conditions to those following his advent, was prepared by the Port Royal school-teacher:

When the days were real cold we were compelled to build a fire in the yard to keep warm. We had a clay chimney which got into such bad condition that we could not use it at all. Whenever it rained we had to cuddle up in the righthand corner of the small building and sit on our books to keep them dry.

Our desks were one straight piece of board with legs on each end, long enough for about five children to sit on with their books in their laps. Coats and hats were placed on a shelf in the rear of the building. Blackboards were made from two wide pieces of board painted black.

For lights we had two windows with the glass broken out, and there was a wooden frame for the blinds. Whenever the days were windy and cold, we had to shut the window and do our work by what light came from the roof.

During the year 1932 we saw two Model T Fords

come up and park on our campus. Four men got out
of the cars and walked around the school building
talking to each other. They came in, measured the
schoolroom and began to work. In a short while they
had laid the foundation of our new school.

In February, 1933, we moved into our neatly built
one-teacher school, equipped with desks and sufficiently
lighted.

One of Mr. Ford's first gifts to these Negro
pupils and teachers, after buildings had been
remodeled and furniture supplied, was to increase the term of instruction from six to nine
months, adding three months to the school
year. Another was that of individual text-
books for each student. Radio sets, stoves,
libraries, night classes, athletic uniforms—have
been among some of the others. Even the
roads leading to the schools have been improved.

One of the Negro pupils tells how Mr. Ford
arranged the gift of textbooks to the Oak Level
School. On his first visit, he remained about
thirty minutes, listening to classes recite. It is
customary for some member of the class, or
the teacher, to hand to the visitor a book containing the recitation, so that he may follow

100

their work. However, with not enough books for the scholars, it was impossible for them to pass one to him. Mr. Ford noticed the difficulty but said nothing. A few weeks later a truck drew up, bringing books for every one.

The significant thing about the Ways, Georgia, project, is that here may be seen again the fulfilment of one of Mr. Ford's ideas—a unique industrial community in the heart of Dixieland —where the combining of industry with agriculture is expected to produce a new and better way of living in America.

Since the industries of the community will obtain their raw materials from products of the soil, experimenting has been carried on in greenhouse culture with many typical plants of the South.

Every industry introduced here must fit the community. At present the chief ones are lumbering, woodworking and agriculture. A lumber-mill and a planing-mill supply the wood used by the students, who, by the way, are being taught to build their own furniture. An important contribution has been a community house with twenty guest-rooms, a large

101

ballroom, lounge, and dining-room. It teaches children to get on socially, and conduct themselves graciously. Old-fashioned dancing is taught them. Each year the Edison Institute orchestra is called to the South, as well as the director of school and dancing activities.

In contrast to the structures that formerly served the Negro children, those constructed or remodeled under Mr. Ford's direction are airy and bright. One of them is the only really modern school for Negro children in the section; it boasts four teachers and a large enrolment. Originally two districts existed, each with a frame school about the size of a freight boxcar. After consolidation, their new building was dedicated in 1931.

VI

During vacation time in the summer, it has been a custom of Mr. and Mrs. Ford to spend part of the season near Huron Mountain on the shore of Lake Superior in Upper Michigan. On this peninsula are large sources of Ford raw materials, including timber and ore; and several important Ford operations. It was inevitable that his ideas on education and industry should find expression here, also.

Adjoining the huge Ford sawmill at Pequaming, a new high school constructed by him opened its doors in September, 1937, with 79 pupils. Being in a lumber town, the school was able to offer shop courses of training along lines of special value to natives of the North woods. Classrooms were provided for home economics and academic courses, together with a library large enough to serve all the residents of the town. An additional unit housed the office and commercial courses, and provided living-quarters for the faculty.

As in the other schools, instruction in vocational and commercial work has been emphasized, and students having special talents may supplement these with individual instruction. The principal heading the faculty of seven came from the State Department of Public Instruction.

Two years previously Mr. Ford gave the community two smaller schools, one for the kindergarten and first grade, another for sec-

103

ond and third grades up to and including the eighth. During 1937 the student body of these elementary schools comprised approximately 125 pupils.

These buildings are spotlessly white, and they have many windows. The grounds are landscaped. Fresh milk is served the pupils during the day as in the other schools. Boys of the fifth, sixth and seventh grades are instructed in manual training; the girls in cooking and sewing. Classes in old-time dancing are held.

During the summer vacation of 1937 vocational instruction, dancing classes, and a recreational program were offered the pupils under the supervision of the faculty, much as at Dearborn. Here, too, summer did not mean a cessation of school activities. Dancing classes met at the Bungalow, the students' social center located in a beautiful wooded setting on the shore of Lake Superior. Such interesting steps as the polka, schottische, mazurka, the rye waltz, heel and toe polka, minuet, standard lancers, and a variety of quadrilles were taught, in addition to the waltz itself.

104

Seventh, eighth, and ninth class girls organized a unit in clothing instruction, and for two hours each day met together and designed and sewed a variety of garments, ranging from dresses, blouses and skirts to pajamas and undergarments.

Girls in the three upper classes studied luncheons. At first they prepared typical luncheon foods; then they combined them by planning and serving several complete meals. An opportunity to act as hostess, waitress, and guest was given each girl.

At the close of vacation the two groups decided to hold a picnic. All the "eats" were planned, prepared, and served by the girls in this foods class.

Equipment of the school foods laboratory in this northern lumber town includes four tables at which two groups of girls may work, each with two two-burner electric plates. Nearby are an electric range and refrigerator. One corner of the laboratory, called "the dining-room," has a dinette table and four chairs. Here the girls serve their meals to their guests.

In the clothing laboratory are four long sew-

105

ing tables with drawers, and six machines, four
of which are electric and two old style. All of
their furniture is made of beautifully grained
birch, and was manufactured in the Ford pattern shop at Iron Mountain, Michigan. One
of the most useful objects is a five-door wardrobe, whose three center doors have full-length
mirrors. By opening two, a triple mirror for
use in fitting dresses is formed. Each compartment of the wardrobe has a rod on which
garments may be hung, and a large drawer for
storing materials and supplies. Venetian blinds
and artificial indirect lighting help to make the
classrooms attractive.

In the woodshop, the machines have been so
constructed that boys of school age may easily
and safely operate them. Among them are cir-
cular saw, jig saw, band saw, grinder, jointer,
sander, wood-turning lathe, drill press, and hollow chisel mortiser. Twelve shop benches
have been provided, together with a tool rack
and lumber rack.

During the summer season as well as winter,
the boys use the shop, their work in vacation
time being purely of a hobby nature. At the

106

end of each session, the chore of cleaning the shop, which includes the cleaning of machines, hand tools, and shop itself, is "bossed" by one of the boys. His clean-up squad is not released until he has inspected the shop, and given it his approval.

Younger boys made for themselves such objects as kites, book-ends, door-stops, corner shelves, tie racks, match boxes, and toothbrush holders. Older boys made furniture of modernistic design—end tables, radio tables, chests of drawers, magazine racks, porch swings.

During the summer of 1937 a program of recreational activities was posted each day. Swimming, horseshoe games, hiking, baseball, excursions, and picnics, were provided under supervision. A new tennis court was constructed.

The highlight of the summer was a visit by Mr. and Mrs. Ford with a party of guests, culminating in dinner served in the new hall by the students and teachers of the home economics department. During the day the vocational departments were in operation, and in

107

the evening an old-time dance was held in the Bungalow.

VII

During the summer of 1937 the Henry Ford Institute of Agricultural Engineering opened its doors in stately Boreham House, near Chelmsford, England, adjoining part of the large farms of Fordson Estates Limited.

Founded "to make available to farmers and farm workers practical and theoretical instruction in applying mechanization to all types of farming, and in use and care of all machinery generally employed," the Institute has been provided with lecture rooms, conference room and workshops.

About thirty-two miles from London, Boreham House was acquired by Mr. Ford when abroad in 1930, to be the center of approximately 1,815 acres of English farmland on which he proposed to conduct experimental farming. The mansion is in the Italian Renaissance style, and more than two hundred years old.

In faraway Fordlandia, 600 miles up the

108

Amazon River, is another Ford school for the children of native workers in the vast rubber project undertaken by Ford. The school building stands on a plateau overlooking the Tapajoz River, and is as modern as any in the United States. Night school is also conducted for adults who wish to improve their status, and is well attended.

A school of still different character is that conducted for convalescent children at the Henry Ford Hospital. These youngsters have been hospitalized for various causes. Some are crippled and attend classes in wheel-chairs. For their instruction and to occupy and improve their minds, the hospital has assigned a regular teacher who adapts the work to the grade of the child and to its strength.

During the summer those children who are able are allowed to tend a small garden tract. Parties are held for them at appropriate seasons such as Halloween and Christmas, with programs to mark the occasions. Frequently entertaining visitors come to break the monotony of the invalid ward. Occasional excursions by bus to points outside the hospital are arranged

109

for those whose health will permit them to make the trip.

Some of the other Ford schools have already received considerable mention. The Henry Ford Trade School was started by Mr. Ford back in 1916 for boys who had been prevented from attending high school because they had to seek employment. The school made it possible for them to learn a trade and receive pay while attending classes. The Apprentice School was organized for ambitious employes who sought instruction in advanced electrical, chemical and mechanical engineering, or in other fields where opportunities exist in the plant.

For young women wishing to become nurses, the School of Nursing and Hygiene was established in connection with the Henry Ford Hospital in Detroit. The students are given instruction and training, and meanwhile reside in the comfortable dormitory rooms of the Clara Ford Nurses' Home.

Nor does this exhaust the subject of Ford educational activities. Mr. and Mrs. Ford's interest in the Martha Berry Schools among the people of the South is well known. On a cam-

110

pus of 25,000 acres, the school's founder created an outstanding project with more than one hundred buildings, devoted to the training of boys and girls into good citizens. Several years ago the Fords presented the school with a group of buildings in Gothic architecture. Two of the wings are named "Clara Hall" after Mrs. Ford and "Mary Hall" after Mr. Ford's mother. A large dining-hall for girls, flanked by girls' dormitories and kindred buildings, stands at the head of an open quadrangle, in which are lovely white-tiled pools.

Another interest nearer home has been in the education of the children of Ford Negro workmen who live in the Michigan village of Inkster. When the first high school structure that he built for them was destroyed by fire almost before it had been placed in use, he replaced it with another. He has also assisted them in remodeling the town high school and authorized the construction of a vocational building for manual training and home economics instruction.

111

Chapter VI

BEGINNING OF THE INSTITUTE

I

*M*ANY VISITORS
among the half-million who visited Greenfield
Village during 1937 inquired about its connection with the Edison Institute. They seemed
puzzled about the set-up as planned by its
founder. "Just what," they asked, "is the relation of the Village to the Institute?" The ex-
planation is a simple one. The Institute pri-
marily is an educational project; it comprises
two units, the Museum and the Village, each
being an integral part. While these units serve
as a laboratory and campus for the school
system, they are also open to the public who
wish to visit the project for their own enlighten-
ment.

It is a mistake to view it simply as a creation

115

to attract and satisfy the curious. Mr. Ford emphasized this when he said:

"Many people seem to believe that Greenfield Village and the Edison Institute and Museum at Dearborn, with their specimens of an earlier type of American life and industry, are just a kind of antiquarian hobby of mine. I do not deny that they have given me a great deal of interest and pleasure. But the project is vastly more than a hobby. It has very definite purposes, and I hope will have results lasting down the years. One purpose is to remind the public who visit it—and sometimes there are thousands a day—of how far and how fast we have come in technical progress in the last century or so. If we have come so far and so fast, is it likely that we shall stop now?"

The project has been variously described, according to its appeal to the person describing it. It has been called "a living epitome of American history—the kind of history unknown to school text-books, for it has small reminder of politics and practically none of wars." Again, it has been hailed as "an engineer's vision of history, not only to be seen but to be

116

heard and felt." It is "the re-creation of a civilization from the objects that it used, its tools, its utensils, and its ornaments."

Mr. Ford's purpose, he has said, is to assemble a complete series of every kind of article used or made in America from the days of the first settler down to the present.

"When we are through," to quote him further, "we shall have reproduced American life as lived; and that, I think, is the best way of preserving at least a part of our history and tradition. For by looking at things that people used and that show the way they lived, a better and truer impression can be gained than could be had in a month of reading—even if there were books whose authors had the facilities to discover the minute details of the older life."

Twelve years ago, when the writer first came in a position to observe the collection, even at that time it had attained vast proportions. Much of the old tractor factory beside the Engineering Laboratory at Dearborn, where during the World War whole shiploads of iron horses were manufactured and shipped to the Allies,

117

was now filled with objects gathered by him from everywhere.

An occasional visitor who was allowed to wander down the long rows of spinning-wheels, Windsor chairs, whatnots, grandfather clocks, melodeons, and countless other objects, often asked: "What is Mr. Ford going to do with all these antiques?"

Few of his subordinates could answer, for Mr. Ford was keeping his own counsel. A lifetime of manufacturing in a highly competitive market had taught him to do so.

It was not as if he had nothing else on his mind. About that time he was planning to discontinue manufacture of the Model T, after nineteen years, necessitating not only the designing of an entirely new Ford car but also the retooling of the Highland Park and Rouge factories.

One day materials arrived from Florida—boards, nails and trim representing a low frame building that had been taken apart at Fort Myers and shipped piece by piece to Dearborn. Some distance behind the Engineering Laboratory in an open field of what had once been a

118

pioneer farm, he instructed his workmen to re-assemble the structure, which had been given to him by his friend Thomas Alva Edison. Indeed, it had been used by the great inventor in Fort Myers for forty winters.

After it had been completed and the furnishings, desk, office chair, letter-press, chandelier overhead, steam engine, boiler and shafting, put in place, he went to a point almost behind the Engineering Laboratory and directed workmen to erect in another open field a square block of concrete, the surface of which had to be reached by ladder from the ground.

On a windy September afternoon in that year 1928, Edison himself, in the presence of a small invited group, mounted the ladder to the surface of the block, where a layer of wet cement had been laid, and thrust into it a spade that had once belonged to their mutual friend Luther Burbank, the great plant wizard, now dead. Thus he symbolized the close union between Industry and Agriculture. In the wet cement he left his footprints as he returned once more to the ladder at the edge of the block, and painstakingly inscribed his name

119

and the date. With this brief ceremony, the cornerstone of what was to be the Edison Institute Museum was laid. About that cornerstone a vast structure covering eight and one-half acres has been constructed.

On the night of the first commencement of high school seniors from the Institute in June, 1937, Mr. W. J. Cameron traced the evolution of the idea as we at Dearborn have observed it:

"When the spot whereon we stand tonight was open field, an invited group stood here one gusty, dusty day in September, 1928, and witnessed Thomas A. Edison inscribe his name in wet cement for the unique memorial in the entrance hall of this building. Probably not one person present had the slightest idea that nine years later on that same ground, we should be graduating a class from a regularly accredited high school. Even now, with the tangible evidence before us, it is hard to realize how much has occurred in the intervening time. We saw you come in and take your places in the intermediate classes; we saw you go on to form the nucleus of a high school; we saw others follow you until the school doubled

120

and trebled and quadrupled its original enrolment; and now you stand on the threshold
of college to be founded here for your further
preparation. It has all occurred so naturally
that only as we look backward and then look
forward can we estimate the value of the idea
that has been unfolding here."

II

On the same afternoon that he inscribed the
cornerstone, Edison turned on steam for the
first time from the boiler in the reconstructed
Fort Myers laboratory. That was the first official ceremony in the field that was later to form
part of the 200-odd acres comprising Greenfield
Village.

By then the two friends had discussed Mr.
Ford's plans and Edison was familiar with what
was in the other's mind. Together they visited
the deserted site of Menlo Park in New Jersey,
where for nearly ten years after 1876 the inventor had toiled, giving to the world the telephone transmitter, phonograph, incandescent

121

lamp, and all the foundations of electric current distribution.

They found the large frame laboratory had been dismantled by neighboring farmers for the lumber salvage it contained. A few brick foundations marked the spot where the machine-shop had stood. Working from these first clues and with Edison's ready assistance, Mr. Ford directed the reclaiming and regathering of materials for the restoration of the Menlo Park buildings.

Some of the original boards were found stored by a farmer. Others were regained through purchase of sheds and other farm buildings. Excavating on the grounds (which Mr. Ford had acquired), diggers brought to light a vast array of relics from Edison's day, ranging from underground wiring for the first electric railroad built there by him in 1880 to the old dump pile where the former workmen had thrown broken and discarded objects. Here was a treasure find such as would have gladdened the heart of an archæologist. All was carefully gathered together and shipped to Dearborn, even the broken bottles and shards.

122

Carloads of red New Jersey clay from the old grounds, together with rocks for foundations, were shipped. Nothing was overlooked, not even the stump of the old hickory tree that once grew near the laboratory.

Mr. Ford sought Edison's advice as to the best source to whom he could go for accurate information concerning the layout of the buildings and furnishings. Edison suggested Mr. Francis Jehl, a former assistant who had worked in the laboratory in 1878-9 and for a time in the early 80's, until he was sent abroad by the inventor to assist in introducing the Edison system in Europe. Mr. Jehl was asked to come to Dearborn and oversee the restoration, and agreed.

The boarding-house near the laboratory where Mr. Jehl and other workmen lived was found intact at Menlo Park, purchased, and dismantled for restoration in a corresponding location in the Village.

Of the two-story brick building that served as office building and library, only one shutter could be found. Mr. Ford arranged to have bricks supplied by the firm furnishing the

123

original ones, and after the structure had been built, placed a single slat from the original shutter in each of those shading the windows of the new office-library.

One building complete in its original features was recovered. It was the little photographic studio in which bulbs for the first successful lamps were blown, and later became known as the "little glass house." It had been located some years previously by the General Electric Company and placed as a shrine in one of the employes' parks. At a ceremony attended by Mr. Edison, the company presented the house to Mr. Ford.

Remnants of the original electric locomotive built by Edison in Menlo Park in 1880 were given by the company, and Mr. Ford set men at work restoring it, as well as duplicating the two small cars it had hauled.

All of these matters were directed by Mr. Ford personally, while at the same time he was arranging for the erection in the Village of other structures.

On a knoll near a bend in the Rouge River he found the highest ground in the Village

124

precincts, and set it aside as a site for the Chapel that he proposed to build in memory of Mrs. Ford's mother and his own mother. In July of that year, Mrs. Ford herself turned the first sod to signal commencement of construction, and the bricks and doors from her girlhood home, the Bryant homestead, went into the building.

After considering what name to give the unique town he was creating, Mr. Ford selected that of the township where Mrs. Ford's home had been. Greenfield Township had been swallowed years before by the spreading city of Detroit, and was no longer on the map. He decided to perpetuate the name by bestowing it on the Village.

III

When Edward Hungerford visited the Village site early in 1929 he wrote:

"There is a pattern to the town. You can see that from the car-window. Men and tractors and teams are scraping and preparing its streets. The clatter of hammers is upon the air. Scaffolding enshrouds buildings, scaffold-

125

ing is being torn from their completed selves.
A gang is laying a railroad track straight up
to a little depot. If you are fifty or more years
old, and came from any small American village,
you will, perhaps, recall such a depot back in
the home town. There are—or were—many
hundreds of them in this land."

To provide a post-office, a search was made
throughout New England for one dating back
to colonial days, and ended in success when one
that had served the people of a little Connecticut hamlet as far back as 1803 was found.
It was brought to Dearborn, with its handmade nails and shutters and hand-hewn laths,
restored, and designated as a government post-
office with its own postmark.

Other buildings were sought, each to illustrate a particular phase of early American life.
An old-time grist-mill, a general store, a shoemaker's shop, a cooper shop, an old carding-
mill—were brought in and set up. To provide
merchandise of the pioneer period for the store,
an emissary searched in upper New York State
and came upon a stock of goods that had been
stored away several generations ago by those

126

who had inherited it. Some of the wares still had on them the old shillings and pence price tags. There were hoop skirts, copper-toed boots, bustles, bolts of cloth, funny round derbies, paper collars and cuffs, red flannel underwear, and such other relics from the days when the general store was the village post-office, grocery, hardware, drug and clothing store all in one. This stock was passed on to Mr. Ford with the understanding that the name of the old gentleman who had once been proprietor, Elias A. Brown, be placed above the store. In accord with this agreement, the name looks down today across the front of the Greenfield Village general store.

Meanwhile a large amount of work was in progress. A paved highway was laid along the Village southern boundary. Gas, water, and electric lines were brought in and made accessible where needed. Streets were laid out and improved. Sidewalks were built; drains dug; gardens planted; fences strung along streets; lawns laid out. On a tract of ground fronting the Chapel which has been set aside as the Vil-

127

lage green and center of activities, large elm
trees were transplanted.

Slowly the village as it had been planned in
Mr. Ford's mind began to take shape. Additional buildings were brought in. For a courthouse, one in which the great Lincoln had
practiced law was sought. One was found in
Lincoln, Illinois, an old Logan county courthouse long since discarded and now being used
as a boarding-house. It was purchased and removed, to be restored and set up on the south
side of the green.

To supply an example of the forerunner of
the American home, Mr. Ford found in the
Cotswold region of England a stone cottage
whose history dated back to the days in the
early seventeenth century when the Pilgrims
sailed to these shores. The modest home was
built entirely of stone; and when it was dismantled and loaded on freight cars for removal
to port, the train was said to have been the long-
est the railroads of England had ever moved.
Two workmen were imported to reconstruct
it in its new site, a shaded spot at the far end
of the village, where a black walnut tree stood

128

● Thomas Edison and Henry Ford inspect ruins of Menlo Park buildings where Edison worked from 1876 to 1885.

● Menlo Park buildings as restored in Greenfield Village.

just as a similar tree had stood in the English setting.

To make the restoration complete Lancashire sheep were brought in to start a flock, for the Cotswold residents had been herders. Pigeons also, and vegetables with which a typically English garden could be planted.

The cottage with its stone floor and centuries-old fireplaces was equipped with furnishings of the period—trestle table, monk's chair, settle, dropleaf table, Bible chest, canopy beds, wooden plates and leather pitchers. It was to illustrate the home from which our forefathers departed when they came to make new homes on the bleak New England shore. A short distance from it, the Secretary House a century younger was subsequently erected by Mr. Ford to illustrate the later type of stately colonial residence.

In 1936 he was given by the Ford dealers of America one of Cape Cod's oldest windmills to include in this end of the Village. More than 7,000 of the dealers came to Dearborn by special trains to participate in the presentation of the gift early in November of that year.

129

The same triangular corner received more additions in 1937—the Plympton house from Woburn, Massachusetts, representing the type of American home that succeeded the log cabin in New England; and the Noah Webster House, which was disposed of to Mr. Ford by Yale University authorities.

IV

But we are getting ahead of our story. We must go back to the beginning of 1929, the year that was to mark the fiftieth anniversary of the invention of the practical incandescent lamp by Edison, October 21, 1879. Mr. Ford invited his friend to commemorate the occasion at the restored Menlo Park in Dearborn, and the inventor accepted.

When the world realized that the birthday of Edison's greatest achievement was nigh, many other interests arranged to join in the celebration. Committees were appointed; the government prepared to issue a special postage stamp bearing a likeness of the first lamp; President Hoover accepted Mr. Ford's invitation to come

130

to Dearborn to dedicate the Edison Institute; Owen D. Young, chairman of the board of General Electric, agreed to act as toastmaster for the evening banquet; facilities were installed to broadcast the event over an international hook-up.

We at Dearborn that summer saw the plans slowly unfold for the dedication. Distinguished visitors came and went, some incognito, others not. All questions were left to Mr. Ford's decision, for it was felt by every one, including Mr. Edsel Ford, that this was to be "his father's party" and his should be the final word on details of the program.

Work on the Logan County courthouse was rushed to complete it in time. Brass screws were used instead of nails to hold the boards of black walnut together. Sackfuls of broken plaster from the original building were emptied to mix with new for the interior walls. "I am restoring this building in such a way that it will stand here at least 200 years," Mr. Ford said.

In September, as has already been related, the first pupils assembled at the Scotch Settle-

131

ment School to inaugurate the Village school system.

Final preparations for the coming dedication began to take shape. Invitations were inscribed and mailed to more than four hundred of the world's leading citizens who might be interested in coming to Dearborn to honor Edison. As soon as acceptances were received, neat booklets containing information as to hotel reservations, transportation to Dearborn, identification cards, and similar data were sent out.

The Village presented a busy scene as workmen hustled about, one crew unrolling large coils of sod across the green, creating a lawn over that large expanse within twenty-four hours; others engaged in painting, hammering, grading, building a tintype studio and so on.

Much work remained to be completed in the new Museum building. Glistening candelabra were hung from the ceilings and given white candles to serve as illumination until after Edison had reenacted the invention of his lamp. Long banquet tables were arranged along the front corridors near the entrance lobby, looking toward the far right where the speakers' table

132

was set. Dignified menu books were printed for the diners. Handsome souvenir books containing descriptive details about the Edison Institute, the Museum and the Village were made ready. Decorative drapes were hung about the banquet corridors.

An old-time railroad train of the 50's was completely restored—wood-burning locomotive, baggage-car and two passenger coaches—and tested on the track between the Rouge plant and the Village depot. The latter, a brick edifice dating to 1860, had been brought to the Village brick by brick from Smith's Creek, Michigan, and reassembled, a gift to Mr. Ford from the Grand Trunk railroad. During a journey to Port Huron with Edison, the inventor had pointed it out as the actual spot where as a news agent fifteen years old, he had been deposited on the platform by an irate conductor for setting the baggage-car on fire.

The interior of the baggage-coach was made to resemble its appearance when the youthful Edison used it as an experimental laboratory between Detroit and Port Huron. Shelves with bottles of chemicals were built against the wall

133

at the front end, and across the aisle was set up a hand printing-press such as he used to publish his paper, *The Herald,* said to have been the first ever issued on a train. A copy of one of the two in existence was obtained, and reprinted for distribution among the passengers, October 21.

V

Edison himself arrived with Mrs. Edison a few days in advance and personally inspected the Menlo Park restoration. When he alighted from Mr. Ford's car at the gate on Christie Street and walked inside the quadrangle bounded by the white picket fence, his eyes fell on the soil.

"H'm!" he exclaimed, pleased. "The same damn old New Jersey clay!"

At the doorway of the old laboratory stood a well-known figure to welcome him.

"Hello, Francis," he greeted Mr. Jehl.

They strolled through the downstairs, where the first little machine-shop had been restored with the old foot-powered machines; saw the photometer room where lamps had been tested

134

for candle power; passed the testing table resting on brick pillars that extended through the
floor to the original foundations; inspected the
chemical nook in which Edison had once been
pictured by an artist from one of the weekly
magazines; looked in the front office with its
high desk and low table. Edison pointed to a
cubbyhole under the stairs. "There's where I
used to go and stretch out sometimes when I
wanted to be alone," he said.

When they had mounted the stairs and he
surveyed for the first time the long room with
its shelves of chemicals and tables of instruments, where he had worked hours, months and
years, he said happily: "Ford, it's 99.9 percent
perfect."

Wondering what detail had been overlooked,
Mr. Ford asked the meaning of the other tenth
of one percent.

"Oh, our floor was never as clean as this,"
Edison chuckled.

Today visitors as they mount the stairs and
view this room exclaim in admiration at the
completeness of the restoration. On the long
shelves that line two walls are bottles and jars

135

containing the same chemicals which once stood here. To learn their identity, Mr. Ford approached the chemical supply house in New York City who had originally supplied Edison. In their old files they uncovered copies of the invoices, and were able not only to furnish the same materials, but also duplicates of the containers.

Most of the instruments on the tables, induction coil, Leyden jars, vacuum pump, and so on, had come as a gift from Edison himself. At the far end of the room stood a small pipe-organ such as once graced the spot, the gift of Hilbourne Roosevelt, uncle of Theodore the First. It served both to aid the hard-of-hearing inventor in his experiments with sound, and to provide music for the midnight suppers of the crew when they worked late. When Mr. Ford found the original had been destroyed, he asked its builders to make a duplicate for him.

In cabinets downstairs and on shelves upstairs stood patent-office models of many of Edison's inventions, priceless in value. They ranged from the first, a vote-recordograph made by him at the age of twenty-one, the stock

136

ticker, the chemical telegraph, the phonograph, the carbon transmitter, the microphone, the electric pen, and a whole series of incandescent lamps starting with the first crude device, with spiral and lever of platinum, mounted on a tall wooden base.

In a front corner of the old telegraph table, Edison seated himself, as often he had sat when he tapped out messages to New York City. "This has followed me all my life," he told Mr. Ford. "First at Newark, then at Menlo Park, next at West Orange, and finally at Fort Myers."

One of the objects of their visit this day was to recreate filaments of cotton sewing thread such as were used in the first successful lamp. They moved to the chest of drawers, a homely gray wooden affair, behind which on a low rostrum Edison had sought his filaments in the old days.

Mr. Ford handed Edison a large gray mortar bowl. "Why, this is our old mortar!" the inventor declared, surprised. "It was broken. How did you get it back?"

Mr. Ford explained how its pieces had been

137

found by the diggers when they excavated the dump pile at Menlo Park. He had taken them home and reassembled them himself, finding all the original segments save one, and that had been replaced.

Edison set it carefully on the corner of the chest. "There's where it always stood," he said. And there it stands today.

Carefully, with his long, graceful, intelligent fingers, the inventor took the strings of thread and carbonized them in a paste. Several he gave to Mr. Ford. Others were taken to mount on stems, later to be housed in glass bulbs, from which the air was to be extracted on a Sprengel mercury pump just as in 1879.

After he had shown them the process, the inventor leaned back in his chair, the same in which he had sat in the old laboratory. Mr. Ford asked a question about the carpenter who had built some of Edison's buildings.

"He lived over in Metuchen," the inventor said, pointing out the window with his hand in the direction of the old town. It was evident that for a moment he fancied himself back in the original laboratory half a century earlier.

138

VI

Although the Saturday and Sunday preceding October 21 had been gloriously sunny with blue skies and white fleecy clouds and the clear, cool tang of autumn, Monday morning dawned with skies overcast and a drizzling rain which continued throughout the day until evening, when it became a downpour. The carefully smoothed streets of the Village turned into lanes of mud such as the early American towns had known only too well. The inclement weather, however, did not dampen the spirits of those who participated.

With the Edisons as their guests, Mr. and Mrs. Ford rode to Rouge Transfer to welcome President and Mrs. Hoover, Secretary George Akerson, Secretary of War James Goode, and other distinguished arrivals who came on the executive's train from the national capital. Accompanying them were newswriters, special correspondents and camera men.

While these boarded the old-fashioned train that was to transport them to the Village, others gathered on the Smith's Creek depot

139

platform to welcome them. During the short train ride, Edison found in the baggage-car a basket such as he had used to purvey his merchandise, and walked through the coaches offering fruit and candies as he had back in 1862. When the train puffed into the Village siding and the others had disembarked, he came down from the baggage-car on specially constructed steps, President Hoover escorting him down. Thus he arrived for a second time on the platform to which he had been unceremoniously discharged sixty-seven years earlier by the conductor.

Ceremonies of the day included inspection of the buildings, luncheon in Clinton Inn at noon, and special events. President Hoover lighted a fire in the fireplace of Logan County courthouse, and Edison lighted one in the old boiler of the brick machine-shop. Neither of these, one symbolizing government and home, the other science and industry, has since been permitted to become extinguished.

The guests roamed about at will. In the general store Julius Rosenwald sat beside the heater with Adolph Ochs and Otto H. Kahn,

140

and reminisced on his experiences as a store-keeper before Sears, Roebuck Company had been launched. On the Inn register appeared such names as Orville Wright, Will Rogers, Will H. Hays, Jane Addams, Walter P. Chrysler, R. E. Olds, Fred P. Fisher, Father O'Donnell, president of Notre Dame, Charles M. Schwab, A. R. Erskine, Roy D. Chapin, John D. Rockefeller, Jr., Charles G. Dawes, George Eastman, Gerard Swope, Lee deForest,—a veritable *Who's Who*.

Special cars transported them back to their hotels to prepare for the evening banquet, which was formal. There was no let-up in the deluge of rain. Those of us who had assisted during the day in explaining the history of the buildings to the guests were soaked to the skin.

But as one stepped into the lobby of the Museum that evening from the drenching outdoors, it was as if one had entered fairyland. All was candle-light. Figures great in contemporary history filed up the broad winding staircase to leave their wraps, then descended to an array of glittering tables that stretched to

141

the right under the brilliant candelabra to the speakers' table.

Madame Curie, co-discoverer of radium, was among the guests. Members of Edison's family, pioneers who had worked with him, delegations from Japan and Europe, giants of the industrial world, leaders of Detroit and the State of Michigan, were numbered at the tables. Messages came from Edward, then Prince of Wales, and Albert Einstein, German scientist. The National and Columbia broadcasting companies brought the program to homes throughout America and beyond the seas.

As the nation sat in candle-light awaiting the moment of the reenactment of the lamp's invention, Edison with the President, Mr. Ford and Mr. Jehl left the hall and drove through the rain into the Village to the restored Menlo Park laboratory, now dimly illuminated by gas flames. Gradually Edison fed current from the glass battery jars to the glistening globe suspended beside the mercury pump, with its filament of carbonized sewing thread.

The tiny horseshoe imprisoned within the globe slowly turned cherry red in the half-light,

142

then brighter and brighter till it reached its blazing maximum. At that moment, the electric lights above the banquet corridors sprang into full brilliance, and everywhere in the homes that had been awaiting the signal, once more the lights were switched on.

President Hoover, in his address dedicating the Edison Institute, closed with these words:

"In establishing this institute, Mr. Ford is doing honor to Mr. Edison in a manner which appeals to a sense of fitness—that is, by founding an institution dedicated to education and scientific research.

"And scientific research means more than its practical results in increased living comfort. The future of our nation is not merely a question of the development of our industries, of reducing the cost of living, of multiplying our harvests, or of larger leisure. We must constantly strengthen the fiber of national life by the inculcation of that veracity of thought which springs from the search for truth. From its pursuit we shall discover the unfolding of beauty, we shall ever widen human understanding.

143

"Mr. Edison has given a long life to such service. Every American owes a debt to him. It is not alone a debt for great benefactions he has brought to mankind, but also a debt for the honor he has brought to our country. Mr. Edison by his own genius and effort rose from modest beginnings to membership among the leaders of men. His life gives renewed confidence that our institutions hold open the door of opportunity to all who would enter.

"Our civilization is much like a garden. It is to be apprised by the quality of its blooms. In degree as we fertilize its soil with liberty, as we maintain diligence in cultivation and guardianship against destructive forces, do we then produce those blossoms, the fragrance of whose lives stimulate renewed endeavor, give to us the courage to renewed effort and confidence of the future."

In replying to the tribute this occasion had paid him, Edison's voice clearly attested the extent of his emotion. He was visibly affected. He spoke briefly as follows:

"Mr. President, ladies and gentlemen, I am told that tonight my voice will reach out to the

144

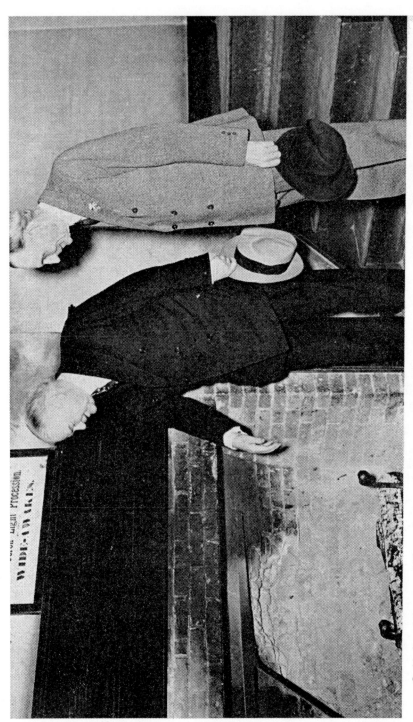

● Herbert Hoover and Henry Ford inspect the fire lighted by the former in Logan County Courthouse, October 21, 1929.

● Cornerstone of museum with Edison's footprints and name, and spade of Luther Burbank.

four corners of the world. It is an unusual opportunity for me to express my deep appreciation and thanks to you all for the countless evidences of your good will. I thank you from the bottom of my heart.

"I would be embarrassed at the honors that are being heaped on me on this unforgettable night were it not for the fact that in honoring me you are also honoring that vast army of thinkers and workers of the past, and those who are carrying on, without whom my work would have gone for nothing.

"If I have spurred men to greater effort and if our work has widened the horizon of man's understanding even a little and given a measure of happiness in the world, I am content.

"This experience makes me realize as never before that Americans are sentimental and this crowning event of Light's Golden Jubilee fills me with gratitude. I thank our President and you all. As to Henry Ford, words are inadequate to express my feelings. I can only say to you that, in the fullest and richest meaning of the term—he is my friend. Good night."

145

VII

The four years following the dedication witnessed the addition of several buildings to the
Village, and the commencement of cataloguing
and arranging exhibits in the Museum. Concrete slabs were laid across the wide exhibition
hall as a foundation for the teakwood which
was to form the floor. Huge ungainly steam-
engines arrived from England and were set up
in one corner. The task of transferring the
collections from the old tractor factory began.

Although it was impractical to permit the
public to wander through the premises while
work was in progress, requests for such permission became so numerous that arrangements
were made to accommodate as many as possible.
Parties who had received such permission assembled in their cars at the Engineering Laboratory, and a procession of about twenty-five
persons left here every fifteen minutes in charge
of a guide. On some days as many as four hundred visitors were escorted over the Village
grounds. None, of course, was admitted to the

146

Museum except on special pass, and then only when peculiarly interested.

Interest in the early American Village continued to grow until by 1933 families were driving into Dearborn from all corners of the compass, only to be disappointed at not being able to enter. During the late spring a thousand or more were turned away daily. Then it was that the officials of the Edison Institute decided to open the Village to the public instead of waiting till it could be completed.

One week later the Museum was also opened to visitors.

Since that time, each year has seen an ever-increasing number touring the Edison Institute. From a maximum of 400 a day, the total has passed 15,000. Every section of the globe has been represented among names in the Inn registry. Most of the great personages of American contemporary life and many foreign notables entered its portals. University presidents, Nobel prize winners, distinguished poets and authors, famous stars of stage and screen,

147

great musicians and singers—have been numbered among its guests.

Prior to 1931, the only hotel accommodations available in Dearborn were small establishments situated at a considerable distance from Village and Museum. As soon as the need for suitable nearby facilities became apparent, Mr. Ford and Edsel Ford decided to meet it by erecting an inn that would be in keeping with the Edison Institute project. The same Georgian style of architecture was selected and a site was set aside opposite the Ford Airport, perhaps half a mile from the Village entrance.

Furnishings of lobby and lounge were chosen in the early American style, with crystal chandeliers overhead and authentic reproductions of historic furniture pieces among those placed in the lobby. The walls of the lounge were decorated with pictorial scenes of colonial and pioneer life in America.

When the Inn had been completed, its management was turned over to an experienced service corporation from New England. Since its opening, it has justified the purpose of the Fords so greatly that during the summer of 1936

148

a dormitory building had to be added to provide quarters for the help; and in 1937 a row of cottages was constructed to supply additional facilities for visitors.

The latter were made as authentic reproductions of historic buildings. Among those thus reproduced were cottages occupied by Walt Whitman, Edgar Allan Poe, Patrick Henry, and Barbara Fritchie.

Chapter VII

THE MUSEUM COLLECTIONS

*V*ISITORS FROM ALL
parts of the globe, from points as far distant as
New Zealand and Iceland, arrive constantly in
Dearborn to view Mr. Ford's unique project.
They approach the grounds through the handsome ornamental iron gateways that mark the
entrance. Lettered in the ironwork is the
date "October 21, 1929" with the name of the
Institute and Greenfield Village.

On the south side of Village Road is a large
parking area where licenses may be glimpsed
on cars from as many as forty different states
and provinces on the same day. Cars from
Maryland and Quebec stand side by side. Despite the size of the accommodations, all of the
space is occupied on busy holidays and cars are

153

parked up and down every available lane in all directions.

On the north side of the Road behind landscaped grounds is the façade of the Museum, reproducing on either side the old City Hall and Congress Hall of Philadelphia, joined to each other and to the reproduction of Independence Hall, the central unit, by long arcades in the same architectural tradition.

Back of this are the libraries, classrooms, laboratories and theater of the Edison Institute, the smaller exhibition rooms of the Museum in which collections of early American furiture, glassware, ceramics, silverware, pewter and musical instruments are on display; and finally, the main exhibition hall with its teakwood floor covering an area of approximately eight acres.

Entrance to the Museum is through the door in the central unit, above which rises a clock tower housing a replica of the Liberty Bell. The building itself is 450 feet by 800 feet, and the front units are connected with the main hall in the rear by five arcades, having open courts between.

The original Independence Square buildings

154

were of handmade brick with base and details of granite, marble and soapstone from the old local quarries. The replicas at Dearborn are built of Harvard handmade red brick, Cold Springs gray granite, a blue-gray Georgia marble and soapstone, all selected to reproduce exactly the appearance of the original. There are ten large entrances, four of which, being flanked with monolithic marble columns in Doric style, are especially impressive.

The main hall is one immense room, broken only by the 180 columns supporting the roof. No ornamental treatment is added, and the necessities of construction and mechanical equipment are relieved only by a refinement in placing and lines. The columns are encased in special steel radiation, part of the modern design. It is lighted from above by unadorned monitors of steel and glass. The transition from colonial days to today is well illustrated by this interior.

Construction of the building was completed during early autumn of the year 1929. The site of the Museum was laid out early in May. By the middle of August the outlines of Independ-

ence Hall could be recognized. On October
21, when the guests gathered for the Institute's
dedication, the front buildings were completed
sufficiently for the staging of the evening's banquet.

II

As the visitor enters the lobby his attention
centers on the cornerstone directly ahead under
glass where Edison inscribed his name, im-
planted the spade of Luther Burbank, and left
his footprints. From the focal point, the corridors lead left and right into chambers containing Philadelphia furniture of the eighteenth
century, placed there as appropriate to the
memorable event that marked Independence
Hall, the signing of the Declaration of Independence in 1776. In the wall-cases are exhibits of glassware and ceramics; on the floor
are exhibition highboys, sofas, secretaries, chairs
and tables. The auditorium of the Institute
opens off the left (or west) corridor. Doors
admit to the lobby, leading into the theater.
In the far corner of the corridor is an exhibit of
early colonial furniture, said to be one of the

156

finest that has been gathered together of that period.

In the Museum collections are some 6,000 pieces of furniture. They go back to European sources of inspiration, carry through to modern times and are finely representative of the craftsmanship of the early American masters—Savery of Philadelphia, Johnson of Salem, Goddard of Newport, Saxon of Boston and Phyfe of New York.

Many of the pieces are of historic as well as intrinsic interest. There are, for instance, a Chippendale table that once was the property of John Hancock; a New England highback chair of 1710, once the property of Lady Pepperell; a corner cupboard owned by Governor Saltonstall of Massachusetts; a Queen Anne chair (1730) owned by General Joseph Warren; a gate-legged table at which Lafayette frequently wined and dined while a guest in the home of Joseph Reynolds at Bristol, Rhode Island.

Noteworthy is the collection of musical furniture. In the sequence of piano-like instruments is a fifteenth-century virginal, which was

157

placed on a table or the player's lap and operated through a little jack which plecked the
strings as the keys were struck. Another "string-
plecking" instrument, a spinet, had a cabinet
of its own—a beautiful piece of craftsmanship,
triangular in form. The harpsichord, of the
type used by Bach, marks a great mechanical
advancement over its predecessors. Also seen
are pianofortes from 1780 on, many of them in
beautiful Sheraton and Duncan Phyfe cases.
And so to the piano, of gradually increasing size
and range of keyboard, and of the square, upright and "grand" types that marked changing
modes and fancies.

Another sequence is that of the organ with
representative types of all periods, beginning
with the so-called "galloper" of lap-melodeons,
with piston keys and piano keys; the "galloper" set on a stand of its own; and thus to
the subsequent metamorphosis of the organ
into a combined musical instrument and piece
of furniture—seraphines, melodeons and har-
moniums—all the reed-types from 1840 on,
many in exquisite cases of mahogany or rose-
wood.

158

In the mechanical group the evolution of the Swiss music-box has been traced, from the smallest types with their tiny steel-toothed brass rolls tinkling tunes from steel combs, to the great multi-rolled instruments, with tympani, organ, trap-drum and bell attachments and their drum-, castinet- and bell-playing automats.

The other musical exhibits include a comprehensive collection of band instruments, gathered by a New York bandmaster. The several hundred pieces in this group, used by famous bands from the Civil War period on, show the evolution of wood-wind instruments, the French horn, saxophone, trombone and other "brass" types, and include the "serpents" which supplied the first "natural" brass in orchestral music.

III

Exhibits in the main hall are arranged in three principal subdivisions or activities, all portrayed by displays of the tools and products of man's industry. The three subdivisions were emphasized years ago in an inscription above the Ford Engineering Laboratory:

> Mankind passes from the old to the new over
> a human bridge formed by those who labor in
> the three principal arts—Agriculture, Manu-
> facture, and Transportation.

Speaking generally, the Agriculture exhibits
are on the visitor's left, at the west side of the
hall, Manufacturing in the center, and Transportation on the right or east side.

Even yet the arrangement of the exhibits in
these three main sections and in the corridors
and wall cases is not permanent. Ever since the
building was opened to the public, visitors have
been privileged to see something most unusual
in Museum technique—the completion and arrangement of exhibits. Ordinarily all this has
been accomplished before the doors are opened.

Unless one actually sees the project from day
to day it is difficult to imagine all that must be
done. Every engine must be in working order.
Gas piping, conduits, air and electric lines must
be brought in wherever necessary before the
final flooring can be laid. Foundations for the
engines, some weighing tons, must be bricked
up. Parts must be machined, restored, polished

160

or sometimes replaced. Progress has been slow but certain.

The general idea in the Agriculture section, tracing the growth of a season's crop, will doubtless be followed when the displays are finally made permanent. Beginning with implements used in preparing the soil, the sequence shows implements for planting seed, for cultivating, for harvesting and finally for the actual preparation of the crop for market.

A glance at some of the exhibits will serve to explain the scope of the collections Mr. Ford has made. Here is a rude wooden plow of the Asiatic type, with a rough-hewn log as its beam, a metal-tipped share and the jaws of oxen as its moldboard. Close by are plows with moldboards sheathed in saw blades, and patented plows—walking and riding—from the Civil War period on, with shares of cast iron and, finally, of chilled steel. Here, too, is the harrow, which rivals the plow in antiquity, from the earliest "bush" types, with square and wheel frames of wood and simple wooden pegs as tines, to the spring-toothed and multiple-disc models of modern times.

161

Many planting and harvesting devices, eloquent of the ingenuity of early American farmers, are shown; scythes, from the first rough metal blades affixed to a tree branch to the cradle scythes—and their mechanical successors, the mowing and reaping machines. There are specimens of Ambler's mowing machine, patented in 1834; a reaper built in the Globe Iron Works in Brockport, New York, in 1848; and a reproduction of the original McCormick reaper—one of the first commercially successful types.

Illustrative of the preparation of crops for market are many flails and mechanical threshing machines, such as the "ground-hog" thresher of a hundred years ago; the horse-powered devices, the portable and skid types, and the engines that enabled steam power to be applied to threshing operations. A Mills engine of 1877 (50 years ahead of its time in the use of superheated steam and forced draught) and the Westinghouse vertical agricultural engine used by Henry Ford in the threshing season 1882, are shown.

Agricultural curiosities supplement the ex-

162

hibit, such as a collection of hay forks, some
with auger-like prongs and others built on the
principle of the iceman's tongs. There are
treadmills, horse-operated, and even dog (or
trained sheep) treadmills devised to relieve the
farmer's wife of the drudgery of operating
plunger churns. Many specimens of the churn
itself in wood and pottery—plunger, rocker,
barrel, paddle and other types—as well as examples of various early cheese presses, are here.

Development of flour milling is traced from
earliest times through the crude Indian stump-
and-stone devices, the mortar-and-pestle crush-
ers and other primitive hand-types to the
European water-powered type represented by
a clumsy but effective Rumanian gristmill.

With the clearing of the land, the lumber
industry sprang into being and out of it
came the wood-working arts. Depicted here are
the tools and machinery they evolved, a characteristic turner's shop in which early home furniture was made, and a cabinetmaker's shop with
specimens of furniture of the Georgian period.
From 1840 on, machine-powered tools came
into use, and the various types of fret saws and

163

band saws with which the over-ornate home furniture of Civil War days was made are shown.

Textiles are allied to Agriculture. The display visualizes major steps in the preparation of flax, cotton, and wool, as well as all types of equipment used in making cloth. The evolution of spinning and its sister art, weaving, is readily traced from prehistoric times to the present through primitive spindles, wheels and distaffs to modern instruments.

Evolution of the flatiron from its crude beginnings through the ingenious mechanical contrivances and the camphene, kerosene and charcoal-heated irons to the modern electrical irons, forms an interesting sequence. Those household implements associated with the flatiron—ironing boards, mangles, washboards, washtubs and washing machines, as well as fluting irons and crimping machines, are shown.

IV

Manufacture—the second division—begins with a steam-engine display; indeed, in the sec-

164

tion may be traced the development of modern efficient steam power. The earliest engine in the exhibit is a Newcomen atmospheric pressure, a reciprocating engine of the walking beam type, developing 11 horsepower. It was used to pump water out of an English coal mine. Serving the engine is a "Haycock" or spherical boiler, so named because it resembled an old-fashioned English haycock. This was the earliest type of boiler used to generate steam to operate engines.

Several other unique engines tower above the other exhibits. A later type of atmospheric pressure engine with an added invention, a separate condensing chamber commonly called a "pickle-pot" because of its shape, is one. This design was called a "Windmill End Winding" engine, or a "whimsey," and was used to draw up coal from mines in England, developing about 19 horsepower.

Alongside is an early reproduction of a Watt, double-acting, rotative engine illustrating the "sun and planet" gear system. The flywheel has 296 wooden mortice teeth which drove two pinions 3 feet in diameter from the shafts of

165

which, motion was used for 43 metal working machines—machines used in lapping or polishing steel ornaments. From this the machine received its name, "lap" engine.

In the rear, reaching almost to the ceiling, is a monster machine—a combination gas-steam engine—rated at 6,000 horsepower, weight approximately 750 tons. Nine of these were used by the Ford Company in the Highland Park plant to develop power when they produced the Model T.

Turning from steam engines to electricity, the visitor sees almost every type of electrical device developed for generating, distributing and consuming. One of the most complete exhibits is the W. J. Hammer collection of 1,100 incandescent lamps. The work of Edison's predecessors in gas and arc lighting is presented. Another important exhibit is a great historic collection of lighting and illuminating devices, one of the most comprehensive in the country, dating back to Egyptian and Roman times. Here are literally thousands of hand-wrought articles used for the creating and dispersing of artificial light: Eskimo lamps; ancient clay

166

lamps; ceramic lamps; Betty lamps; lamps that burned whale oil, camphene, kerosene; store lamps, mine lamps, carriage lamps; petticoat lamps; hanging lamps and swinging lamps; tallow, wax and bayberry candles; rush lights; candle-holders; candlesticks—wood, stone, bone, shell, glass and every known metal or combination of metals; chandeliers and sconces; tinder-boxes and pistols; and all the gadgets associated with artificial lighting, such as snuffers, trays and matchholders.

We find here the evolution of the vacuum cleaner (which stems back through the carpet-sweeper of "Brussels Carpet Days" to the corn brooms and brushes of the colonists) ; of heating and cooking devices (open fireplaces, early baseburners and Franklin stoves; kerosene, gas and electrical ranges) ; of refrigerating equipment; and of mimeographs, dictaphones, typewriters, mailing machines and scores of other devices that constitute the familiar machinery of our everyday lives.

Among these is the camera sequence, which shows its development through Edison's kinetophone and kinetoscope, forerunners of motion

167

and talking picture machines, to the modern equipment of the motion picture industry.

Back of the form of "graphic art" is the art of printing. So we have a chronological development of the machinery of printing, shown in models of the wooden hand press of Blaeu, the Columbian hand press, the Washington hand press and early platen presses operated by treadle, with representative works of the printing art in the form of broadsides, pamphlets and tracts, and numerous specimens of typography as well as early examples of type casting and type founding.

One exhibit includes a section of every cable stretched across the Atlantic, commencing with the first laid by Cyrus Field in 1858, which failed, and the second, laid by the Great Eastern between Ireland and Newfoundland, which was a success.

The works of the great physicists who preceded Edison in the field of electrical discovery and invention are not neglected in the museum exhibits. Nor are his great contemporaries overlooked—Nikola, Tesla, Steinmetz, Westinghouse and others.

168

V

The section of the hall showing Transportation includes all types of locomotion and shows reproductions of chariots found in ancient tombs, original primitive ox sledges, ox carts with solid wheels, and wagons and carriages of every description. Power locomotion is shown through gasoline, steam, and electric automobiles; airplanes, motorcycles, boats, bicyles and locomotives.

Of American-made horse-drawn vehicles— both those that are purely American in character and those of foreign derivation—there is a wealth of fine examples. In the first class are included the colonial gig, chaise and chair; the buckboard; the tin peddler's cart; the rockaway, a smart closed vehicle with an overlapping roof for the protection of the driver; and a beautiful example of coach, built by William Ross in 1760 and used by General Lafayette during his first visit to this country. In the second class are hansom cabs, broughams, victorias, landaus and the Cuban volante. There

is also a full sequence of sleighs and cutters de-
riving from the earliest sled.

Paralleling this is a comprehensive display of
fire-fighting equipment, through which the
evolution of the fire engine is traced from the
first crude devices pumped by hand and pulled
by volunteer power, to the gorgeous horse-
drawn and power-driven engines of our youth
and the self-propelled motorized units of the
automobile age.

Early coaches that mark epochal steps in the
advancement of design and construction are
seen. The Conestoga Wagon, a purely American product made in Conestoga Valley in Lancaster County, Pennsylvania, has a prominent
corner of the display.

Airplanes as an important phase of transportation are represented by a 1909 Bleriot; the
"Pride of Detroit," which flew around the
world; an Autogyro; Admiral Byrd's North
and South Pole planes, a Fokker and a Ford.

The track spurs in the Museum floor contain the development of the locomotive, the
earliest being a replica of the "Rocket" which
was the first successful steam locomotive, built

170

in England, October, 1829. The chronology follows to the "DeWitt Clinton," built in 1831, the first practical locomotive in America, a reconstruction of the original. Following are locomotives of the Civil War period—wood burners of 1860 and 1865—and one dated 1897. The largest engine, built in 1902, was the first to attain a speed of more than 90 miles an hour. A French engine built for narrow-gauge tracks and a modern engine, 1915, complete the chronology.

On one of the tracks is the old-style train on which Edison and Mrs. Edison, escorted by the then President Herbert Hoover and Mrs. Hoover, Mr. and Mrs. Henry Ford and other guests, rode to Greenfield Village to take part in Light's Golden Jubilee celebration and the dedication of the Institute.

The evolution of cycling is depicted in an infinite variety of models, from von Sauerbronn's crude draisine or "Gentleman's Hobbyhorse," propelled without benefit of pedals, to the latest type of modern motorcycle, and including the "Boneshaker"; the "phantom" of the 60's; the "spider" of the 70's; the high-

171

wheeled racing "ordinaries" and "extraordinaries" of the 80's, with small wheel behind or before; the so-called "safety" bicycles of the twentieth century; tamdems, four-seaters and one freak, beloved of small boys, that has 10 seats.

In the bicycle exhibit, the visitor may see the largest and smallest bicycles ever built and used.

The automobile sequence is comprehensive, both in its foreign and American types, with examples of the Daimler, the Benz, the Eisenach and others built from 1884 to 1902, a model of the first Isotta-Fraschini and an early Renault. The early American makes include the Winton, Haynes, Cadillac and Reo, various "electrics" and the steamers of Stanley, White and others.

The story of the Ford automobile is told from the first Model A of 1903, through subsequent developments of the Model T, represented by the 15,000,000th Ford car, and the later Model A, represented by the 20,000,000th. It includes the Model K—the only six-cylinder model ever built in the Ford factories—as well as the famous Ford racing cars—the "999," the

172

"Seven-by-Seven Opposed" and the "Model T Hill-climbing Racer" of 1910.

Among the cars in the transportation exhibit that attract attention is Riker's "Bullet," a streamlined, skeleton car of ancient vintage which, powered by storage batteries, challenged all-comers (steamers, electric, gasoline-powered cars, etc.) to a test of speed and won the first automobile race in this country.

In the northeast corner of the exhibition hall stands a reconstruction of the historic Caleb Taft Blacksmith Shop, Uxbridge, Massachusetts. The shop contains one of the few remaining ox slings in which the ox was fastened and then lifted by a winch so the smith could shoe the beast. The poet Longfellow knew of this shop and occasionally visited it. Other articles include a wooden frame forge with hand-operated bellows, benches for nail makers and a stone-weighted, hand-operated drill, the first type of pressure drill.

One of the fascinating sections of the Museum is a typical old-fashioned street that is lined with replicas of old stores and shops. This method of exhibiting some of the collections and the paraphernalia used in connection with them by early craftsmen has made it possible to assemble within handy confines and in an appropriate setting all the features comprising a display.

Those already arranged by the close of 1937 included, in addition to those mentioned: a Mariner's shop, Tinsmith, Pewterer, Candlemaker, Toys, Barber, Millinery, Photographer, Cobbler, Combmaker.

In a corner of the pewter shop is a caldron for melting the alloy. Nearby is the foot-power lathe for burnishing, and about the shop are plate and spoon molds of bronze. The pewter on display in the window and on the shelves along the side wall is from the last period of general use.

The tinsmith's shop was modeled after one kept by J. B. Sweet at Pittsfield, New Hampshire, and is equipped with tools to turn out almost any article in small tinware.

In the candle-maker's shop are illustrated the two most common methods of making candles, the dip and mold. Two types of dip are shown,

174

one being built like a scale with weights to balance the candles and regulate their size; and another representing the rotary type. Candle molds are shown on work benches, along with other examples of candle-making equipment.

Chapter VIII

GREENFIELD VILLAGE

I

*A*FTER MEIGS O.
Frost visited Greenfield Village in the summer of 1934, he returned to New Orleans and
described it as a great poem, an American epic,
written with wood, stone, earth and steel. Much
as those who serve within its gates love its rest-
ful beauty and its refreshing inspiration of the
American tradition, they often gain from en-
thused visitors a new conception of Mr. Ford's
creation.

Forgotten memories are brought back, and
faith in America's great destiny is wakened
anew.

Admittance to the Village is through the
Gate Lodge, a structure in Georgian architecture in keeping with the Museum and Institute
buildings. Once past its doors, the visitor is

179

free to wander at will down the streets and by-paths of yesterday. Occasionally a hack, landau, or station bus rattles past, sometimes loaded with passengers, sometimes empty. A horse-drawn water wagon rolls by, sprinkling the dust. A white-coated street cleaner with broom pushes a wheeled cart.

Facing the visitor as he walks down Main Street is a rounded hillock of lawn, framing a floral clock that once stood in Detroit Waterworks Park, a favorite landmark of the 90's. When the authorities decided it was too expensive to keep up, Mr. Ford arranged to transplant it into the Village. Long, thin white hands record the passing hours, slowly swinging across the green dial past the red Roman numerals. They are formed by approximately six thousand plants imbedded horizontally into soil six inches deep, and held in place by chicken-wire. During the winter, these are removed and a painted face, closely resembling that formed by the plants, replaces them till spring comes again.

That part of the Village directly before the visitor is the industrial section, devoted largely

180

to mills. At his left at the rear of the Institute are two old-time sawmills, one equipped with vertical saw and another with horizontal. Some of the lumber used in the Village is sawed here, and good-sized logs are often piled here as in the old days awaiting their turn.

The oldest of these mills goes back more than a century, and was originally operated by water power when it stood near Monroe, Michigan, on the banks of Stony Creek. It was erected there by one Loranger, an early settler who had migrated to lower Michigan from Quebec, and whose land grant was signed by John Quincy Adams.

Adjoining the sawmill is a large mill-like structure whose roof looks out above the surrounding buildings. Its sides are drab and unpainted; they are broken by large windows. Attached to it are two small annexes, a greenhouse and a brick room that serves as an experimental laboratory.

Despite its uninteresting appearance, this building has played a unique role. Within its walls young men of the Ford Motor Company performed the first experiments with farm

181

products, looking toward a closer link between agriculture and industry terminating in the selection of the soybean. These experiments and their results are described in more detail in a succeeding chapter.

In the rear of the "Chemical Plant," as it is called, is another small frame structure which houses the oil extraction equipment designed for use in connection with the soybean. This also is a temporary building, for the production processes, once definite results had been obtained, were transferred to the Rouge Plant.

When the visitor enters the Village through the Gate Lodge entrance, he usually follows a route leading eastward on Main Street, with sawmills, "Chemical Plant" and Barn on his left. Shortly he reaches the Loranger gristmill, a small white building which was once operated by the same Loranger beside the sawmill on Stony Creek. Today it grinds flour and meal by the stone burr process as it did one hundred years ago. Two of the original millstones lie on the grass outside the building. Instead of the original water-wheel, a steam engine now supplies power, but the product is much the

182

same and in large demand. Indeed, this is one of the industries of the Village that may be said to be most nearly self-supporting.

Here is illustrated one of the significant lessons of the Village. Industry was on a smaller scale a century ago, when two or three men were a complete force for this mill. Yet it was able to provide the domestic requirements of the population found within several miles of a town of this size. The men who worked in such a mill were closer to the soil, and the materials they worked with were closer to the soil. They looked to themselves for a means of livelihood rather than to an employer. When the mill shut down, as it did occasionally, they were all able to fend for themselves. They did not live in apartments nor on twenty-five-foot lots. All had gardens and chickens; some had cows. There was no destitution such as is seen today in large industrial centers during slack periods. The workers had double security—the job at the mill, and the tract of ground beside their cottage.

Beyond the Loranger gristmill is the Village machine-shop in which parts and engines for

183

use in Museum and Village are machined and restored. It was named in honor of Armington and Sims, a firm that supplied high-speed steam engines to Edison for his direct-connected Jumbo dynamos when he lighted New York City for the first time. Many relics are here to commemorate their work—drafting-board, drawing-tools, catalogs and records.

Bagley Avenue, the next street intersection, was named for a similar street in downtown Detroit where Mr. and Mrs. Ford lived for several years when he was a steam engineer employed by the Detroit Edison Company. Facing the street is a small brick shed that once stood behind their house at 58 Bagley Avenue. The shed was made over by Mr. Ford into a small machine-shop where he could work on his idea for a horseless carriage powered by a 2-cylinder gasoline engine.

In this very shed he finished his first car, using bicycle wheels, plumbing pipe, carriage cushions, and such other equipment as he could gather together or make himself. When he was ready to take it out for a test run, he found it would not go through the door. Consequently

184

the door on the right is wider than that on the left, made so by him so that the car could be wheeled into the alley.

When, after he had been persuaded to restore the brick shed in the Village, the Institute decided to undertake advanced experiments, no building could be found more appropriate to the purpose than the one in which was made the first Ford car. Since that time the shed has been closed to the public, to prevent interruption of the experiments.

In this same general vicinity are several industries in actual operation, and others preserved as reminiscent of earlier times. On the left behind the Armington and Sims Machine Shop is the Lapeer Shop where furniture for Village and Museum is restored by expert workmen. It also contains benches and tools for boy students of the Village who are interested in manual training, except those of the McGuffey School, who have their own little shop. Because of the nature of work performed here and the objection to constant interruptions, visitors are not encouraged to enter this building unless specially interested.

185

Beyond is the Sandwich glass plant, a favorite structure to both young and old. Within, a glassblower and apprentices make chemical apparatus for sale to the Ford company, the Henry Ford Hospital, or the schools, as well as many small souvenirs that are in much demand by visitors. The building gets its name from the fact that it contains the few remaining relics of the original glass plant that once served at Sandwich, Massachusetts.

Some distance away, near the extreme northwestern corner of the Village, are the brickyard and pottery, part of a ceramics group. Although these structures have no historical significance, they preserve the earlier methods of manufacturing. In the pottery may be seen the old hand-operated "kick" wheel. Here, too, souvenirs are made for visitors, and pupils of the Village schools learn the craft.

Two other mills are illustrative of the textile industry in the early American scene. They are the Hanks Silk Mill and the Plymouth Carding Mill. The former was found on a Connecticut stream, where, as the first powered silkmill in America, it reeled thread as long

186

ago as 1810. Water power has given place to steam, but the earlier wooden machinery has been reconstructed from patent-office drawings. Silkworms have been bred from eggs and fed on mulberry leaves gathered from trees near Dearborn. Several attempts have been made to grow trees in the Village precincts, and may in time prove successful.

It was to the Plymouth Carding Mill that William Ford, father of Henry, hauled his wool after shearing, to be carded into long white skeins for spinning. At that time it served all the countryside of western Wayne County. Today it cards wool as of yore, and also provides a variety of looms for weaving, from foot-powered Jacquard looms to the most modern. Much of the work for village buildings has been done here. The carpet in the aisles of the Martha-Mary Chapel, and the fabric for the pew seats were woven here. So were the carpets in rooms of the Stephen Foster House. Products of the mill are in much demand as souvenirs.

In the rear, inaccessible to visitors, is the Weave Shed where girl pupils of the Village

187

schools operate their looms, forming patterns and producing merchandise that has a ready sale.

The intersection of Washington Boulevard and Main Street is one of the busiest corners in the Village. Even during the years when new structures were being moved in, it was a center of activity. For one thing the Owl Lunch Wagon stands here, having been brought from its old site in the heart of downtown Detroit where it dispensed midnight snacks to late workers, politicians, newspapermen, police officers, and others. In its new home it continues to serve frankfurters, hamburgers, milk and coffee as a convenience to visitors. In its shade are benches for those who wish to sit down and rest while they dine.

Alongside the Owl Lunch Wagon is the Village Fire Department, a shed housing a hand-operated hose cart and fire engine. On the roof is an alarm bell that once called volunteers to man the engine. Above the doors is the descriptive appellation "The Deluge." The suction engine once served in the poet Whittier's native village. Of it he is said to have

188

written: "The engine wet all around but spared the fire."

II

Spreading fanwise from the intersection, rows of early craft shops fill most of the intervening space between here and the Village green. Like the mills, these shops revive industries that are fast vanishing from the American scene. Others combine crafts with commerce, or commemorate a historical personage.

One block south of Main Street is a group of buildings, two of which have to do with watches, clocks and watchmaking; while two others honor the inventions and discoveries of the Wright brothers.

Just off Bagley Avenue is a dark red brick store of the 70's, once the store and watch-shop of Robert Magill at 444 Baker Street, Detroit. A rear room has special interest. Within it at a bench, in the winter of 1879, worked 16-year-old Henry Ford, cleaning and repairing timepieces. The story is that he obtained employment here four hours a night to supplement the

189

weekly wage earned by him during the day at a Detroit machine-shop.

This did not mark the beginning of his interest in watches—as a mere boy he had kept all those of the neighborhood in repair. Mr. Magill feared his customers might doubt so youthful a workman could make their repairs expertly, hence the stool at the bench in the rear room out of sight.

Some of the tools used by the youthful Henry while working for Mr. Magill were made by him at the Dearborn farm. He had a screwdriver which he made from a shingle nail; a pair of tweezers made from a corset stay; and he also used knitting needles to make other tools.

One block east of the Magill Shop is a jewelry-store and watch-shop of more pretentious type. Sir John Bennett, of 65 Cheapside, London, held watchmaking appointments to royalty—indeed, his firm is still famous today in the English metropolis.

Above the doorway in an alcove stand figures of two giant effigies known as "Gog and Magog." Each quarter-hour they announce the

190

time, aided by an angel and Father Time, striking the Westminster Chimes with hammers on
differently toned bells. Exhibits of clocks extending back as far as 1630, of silverware, of
jewelry ranging from cameos to lorgnettes, and
of watches of many different styles and works,
fill the mahogany wall cases and counters.

In the large upstairs room above the store,
experienced watch and clock repair men have
their tools and benches. They restore music-
boxes and many other objects requiring the
skilled attention of master craftsmen.

During the year 1937 two new structures
were moved into the Village and placed in the
block opposite the Magill Shop and extending
to Washington Boulevard, to form a shrine to
Wilbur and Orville Wright. Representatives
of the Institute, assisted by the Early Birds, an
organization of pioneer flyers, arranged to purchase the two-story brick store in which the
Wright cycle business was carried on in Dayton,
Ohio. After the structure had been dismantled and restored in the Village, much of
the machinery used by the brothers in making

191

their first airplane was found and replaced in the shop.

Next came the dwelling that stood on Hawthorne Street in Dayton, birthplace of Orville Wright in 1871 and the boyhood home of the brothers. Restored, it was placed in an expanse of lawn adjoining the shop and equipped with furniture used by the Wrights in the former days.

East along Main Street from the boulevard, another cluster of shops in which the pioneer crafts could be carried on was placed. In the shade of a spreading chestnut tree stands a stone blacksmith-shop. The horses used in Village activities are shod within, and serve to keep the smith and his apprentice occupied. Forge and anvil are at the left of the door. Sparks fly, and the anvil's ring may be heard for a considerable distance.

Next door is the oldest craft shop in the Village, a New Hampshire cooper-shop dating back to 1787. In colonial times the cooper built watertight hogsheads for commerce, barrels for shipping fruits or vegetables, buckets for maple sap, and wooden pails for every

192

home. Today in the same shop, an experienced cooper and his apprentice make smaller articles, fastening them without glue or nails, binding staves together with hickory hoops, fitting the bottoms into grooves on the sides. Its great semicircular fireplace, the largest in the Village, was used to dry green wood and stout oak casks.

As the visitor approaches Christie Street he encounters two shops of the early shoemaker's craft, both from the Merrimac Valley. The Toll House Shoe Shop on the corner was built about 1828 on the banks of the Merrimac where a covered bridge crossed from Rocks Village to West Newbury. Tolls were collected by the shoemaker from those desiring to cross the bridge, as witness the chart of toll charges hanging on the south wall of the shop.

The poet Whittier frequently visited the spot, and in his poem *The Countess* mentioned——

> The tollman in his cobbler's stall
> Sits smoking with closed eyes.

Today may be heard the rat-a-tat-tat of the shoemaker's hammer as he sits in the stall,

193

shaping his products by hand. In addition to light, flexible oxfords, he makes leather souvenirs for visitors.

Illustrative of the days when farmers of New England made shoes during the winter season as a sideline is the shop next to the Toll House Shoe Shop. More than sixty years ago it was used by William Currier, who, like hundreds of others, found it serviceable in cold weather. It was one of the first to be equipped with machines. A steam engine drove the stitching machine and buffer. Thread processed in a small vat of homemade wax, warmed by a kerosene burner, the rack upon which shoes were dried (they were sewed together wet, being more pliable), cutting patterns, and a leather-splitting machine formed part of the equipment. Currier was an industrious craftsman, working by the light of a kerosene lantern when daylight failed.

Around the corner from the Toll House Shoe Shop is a Tin Type Studio where the almost lost arts of the tintype, daguerreotype and ambrotype flourish as they did for earlier generations. The old-time tintype artist is a

194

character in himself. Many of the world's great have sat before his camera and auto-graphed tintypes for the glass galleries on the studio walls. After much research and experi-menting he has revived the art of making daguerreotypes, one of the few men in the world today able to perform that art with per-fection. The equipment used by him was re-covered from trunks in old garrets.

III

Christie Street, so named because it borders the Menlo Park rectangle as did the original Christie Street of the New Jersey hamlet when Edison toiled there, is the principal north and south thoroughfare of Greenfield Village.

In addition, it might be said to trace the thread of the inventor's career. The street be-gins at Smith Creek depot, at which as a youth of fifteen Edison was discharged by the irate conductor. Proceeding southward, it parallels a white picket fence surrounding Menlo Park, scene of his world-changing inventions. Be-yond, it passes Sally Jordan's boarding-house

195

where so many of his associates lived, and where he laid his wires to introduce use of the incandescent lamp. Finally, it terminates at the Fort Myers laboratory, scene of his final experiments, those seeking to produce rubber from the goldenrod.

Wandering along Christie Street, one senses a commingling of objectively historical and warmly personal associations such as has already been experienced in visits to the mills and craft shops.

Directly at the corner is a small white dwelling whose white columns betray its connection with that period in Michigan history when Greek influence was felt not only in architecture but in the names of Ypsilanti and many other towns. Removed to the Village from its original site in Plymouth, Michigan, the house has served as the headquarters of the architect.

Next door is a low white clapboard building —the Village post-office. Erected when Thomas Jefferson was president, it was the gathering-place for citizens of Phoenixville, Connecticut, for more than a century. Its door and shutters are made of two layers of wood fastened with

196

hand-forged nails to prevent warping. Hinges, latches, iron bars for the shutters, and hooks to hold them back are original handmade fixtures.

Over the door is a sign—"F. I. C."—Fire Insurance Company. Hand-split laths, rough and unfinished, show through an unplastered section of wall on the inside. Postcards mailed here go out with the postmark of "Greenfield, Michigan," for this is an official government post-office.

On October 21, 1929, when it was first opened, Edison received between six hundred and seven hundred letters here. The first letter to go through it was a Special Delivery to former President Hoover.

At the opposite end of the building is an apothecary-shop, where hang prescriptions dating back more than a generation for medicines long since used. Rows of drawers containing musty herbs line the wall. On shelves are flamboyant bottles of nerve vitalizer, heart remedy, rheumatic syrup and lung balm. Atop a case is a jar for leeches and tall bottles of colored water that symbolized the apothecary's trade. On the left is a counter with a small display

197

case of perfumes at one end, and a screen back of which the chemist mixed his cures at the other. A small glass peephole enabled him to keep an eye on customers.

After leaving the post-office, Christie Street reaches the Village green to form the west boundary, or foot of the common. It passes the green-shuttered Town Hall School, with porch supported by white Ionic columns. Beyond, at the southwest corner of the green, it passes the brick Menlo Park Machine Shop, first of the buildings in the Edison quadrangle.

For the space of an entire block it follows along the picket fence that encloses the buildings, past the little house where bulbs for the first lamps were blown, past the "dump" and its display of rescued relics, till it comes to the gate admitting to the office and library. During all this time at its right has loomed the gray two-story structure used by the inventor as his laboratory. On its left, behind a screen of shrubbery, are the McGuffey buildings facing on the other lane.

Leaving the group, it extends to another fence which encloses grounds and garden of

198

Sally Jordan's boarding-house. Because that house is used by the McGuffey pupils at noon for lunch, it is not shown to visitors. However, passersby may note the outside wiring that leads from the helmetted street lamps to the porch light and on into the house. Incidentally, close examination of the street lamps will reveal old-time wooden sockets and cardboard filament bulbs such as Edison used in 1880 for his public demonstration.

Beyond the boarding-house is the Fort Myers laboratory marking the end of the street. At this point the walk turns eastward and leads up to the shaded lane where the Village homes stand among the pine, elm and maple trees.

IV

As in the traditional early American community, the public buildings of Greenfield Village—the Inn, the Chapel, the School, the Courthouse, the General Store, and the Town Hall—are centered around the Village green.

At the head of the green dominating the landscape with its colonial classic façade and its

199

Christopher Wren spire, Martha-Mary Chapel is easily the most important structure in the Village. In addition to serving for the morning exercises of the school pupils, it provides a place on Sunday for a brief service arranged and conducted by the guides of the Village. Non-sectarian in character, the program includes selections by a choir organized among the young men of the staff, an occasional solo, and a prose or poetic reading from one of the humbler American poets or one of the world's masterpieces. Started originally to provide a period of reflection and worship for the Village on Sunday mornings, it attracts many visitors both from those in the Village for the day and from residents of nearby Dearborn.

The building itself was copied largely from a church in Bradford, Massachusetts. The clear-toned bell in its spire was cast by a close relative of the great Paul Revere. With its name, commemorating those of the mothers of Mrs. and Mr. Ford and its bricks and front doors from Mrs. Ford's girlhood home, it offers many sentimental associations to the founder of the Village and his wife.

200

In one of his Sunday evening radio talks, Mr. Cameron related an incident connected with the Chapel. Some one asked Mr. Ford if he and Mrs. Ford had been married in a church. "No," said he, and then quickly: "Yes! Yes! I was! That is, I was married in Mrs. Ford's girlhood home; but its bricks and doors are now part of Martha-Mary Chapel, so, after all, I *was* married in a church."

Concealed behind the walls is a great pipe-organ. Visitors may sit in the tall-backed, white-painted pews with their mahogany top-rails, and listen to the rich tones of a favorite hymn. Mr. and Mrs. Ford have sat there and heard their mothers' favorite hymns played thus. It dawned on Mr. Ford that others would love the same privilege. So now, daily, a student trained as an organist sits to play any hymn on request. Often silent tears creep down the cheeks of listeners at memories that come flooding back as they hear once more the soft melodious strains of a dearly loved tune.

Clinton Inn, at the north side of the green, is a typical Michigan hostelry of a hundred years ago. A row of white Doric columns supports an upper balcony and frames a wide porch across the entire front of the building. The interior is furnished as it was when the tavern hospitably offered night lodging to stagecoach travelers journeying between Detroit and Chicago before the days of the railroad. The old barroom, the comfortable everyday parlor with rag carpet and whatnot, the meticulously Victorian Sunday parlor with its horsehair furniture, lace curtains and brass andirons, the wide kitchen with its smoke-darkened ceiling, its broad fireplace and its hundred-odd household utensils, form a textbook on life in the early part of the nineteenth century.

Because the pupils of the Village schools, except the two lower grades, are served a hot lunch at noon in the dining-room of the Inn, it has been closed to the public for one hour during the noon period.

Upstairs is a "spring" ballroom, whose floor still sways to the cadence of dancers' feet when classes of pupils step through old-time dances to the strains of the Institute orchestra playing on old-time instruments.

202

Behind the Inn is a typical vegetable garden, and back of that is a red livery stable with gambrel roof and weathervane. The horses used by pupils of the riding classes are kept in this building.

Like the Inn, the general store is also an early Michigan structure, having been brought from Waterford, where it served for nearly a century. To many, this is the most interesting building in the Village, reminding them of countless early memories. Counters stretch back from the front doors on either side. Those at the left contain elixirs, china doll heads, comic valentines, Noah's arks, slate-pencils, and similar objects. On the shelves are glass jars holding peppermint stick candy or horehound. Glass lamp chimneys line a rack overhead; chests of tea and spices crowd the top shelves; soap dishes and match boxes appear. Screened cheesebox, peanut roaster with tiny kerosene lamp, fly trap, coffee grinder, cracker barrel, sugar box . . . invite the delighted exclamations of the sojourner.

In the rear is the hardware department. Its wares range from buggy whips to square hand-

203

made nails, and wooden buckets. On the opposite side are the drygoods, jewelry and millinery departments. Carpet-covered stools front the counter for the use of women customers. On display is everything from satin bow ties large enough to cover a shirt front to wooden button molds, tarnished shirt-waist sets, and natural-hair "rats." In the street in front of the store is a row of well-gnawed hitching-posts and a lozenge-shaped street corner lamp.

Directly across the green from the store stands the Logan County Courthouse, tall and rectangular. Here in one room is the start and finish of Abraham Lincoln's life. Here he commenced the practice of law as a young man. Against the wall are a few of the rails said to have been split by him. And in a corner is a red plush rocker in a glass case, wherein he sat on that night at Ford's Theatre in Washington in 1865, when an assassin's bullet brought death to the weary president. The faded rose and gold upholstery at its back is stained yet with his blood.

In the shadow of the building between it and the Menlo Park corner are two slave huts

204

brought north from the Hermitage, near Mr.
Ford's plantation at Ways, Georgia.

V

One of the purposes of the early American
Village is to portray the development of the
home and of life within it through the generations. As a people we know a little about antiques, but hardly anything about the life of
that earlier America which produced them.
One reason is that books and pictures cannot
describe it so that it seems to live on the written
page. It is difficult to share the life of those
days by reading in an easy-chair under the light
of an electric lamp.

By presenting the actual objects in use,
Greenfield Village makes it possible for even
the unimaginative visitor to reconstruct the
methods of living of his forebears. He may see
how they cooked their meals, he can see for
himself the rope spring beds and the trundle
beds on which they and their children slept,
he can see their methods of using the candle
molds with which they made their evenings less
completely dark.

The section of the Village directly before the visitor after he leaves Christie Street is largely devoted to tracing the development of the American home, and forms one of the most truly charming portions of Greenfield. A tree-shaded country road passes along the edge of a low ridge where the lovely homes stand among the trees.

Many different generations in as many different scenes have passed through the years with these homes as their habitations. The limestone English Cottage of the early seventeenth century, an abode of shepherds; the small frame house that Puritan settlers built in Woburn, Massachusetts; the eighteenth century mansion that stood on Secretary Hill in Exeter, New Hampshire, the residence of a Secretary of State; the impressive home in which Noah Webster, lexicographer, first saw the light of day in New Haven, Connecticut; the architectural gem from Ann Arbor, Michigan, in which Robert Frost lived while lecturing on an honorary fellowship; the low rambling homestead from western Ontario built by Edison's grandfather a century ago, in which the

206

inventor's father and mother were married; the tall unpretentious dwelling from Lancaster, Massachusetts, where Luther Burbank, world famous plant wizard and friend of Edison and Ford, was born in 1849; the simple, stately Stephen Foster House of the early nineteenth century, looking down upon the Suwanee River. . . .

First of these to be viewed by the visitor as he mounts the ridge and reaches the lane is the Stephen Foster House built about 1815. A brick walk leads up to a classic doorway with pointed portico. The house seems to consist of a single story, low-roofed, white with green shutters. The door opens into a wide hall that stretches entirely across the ground floor from front to rear. On the left is the music-room; a portrait of the composer hangs over the fireplace, and an electric organ stands at one side against the wall. Amplifiers carry the sound to all parts of the edifice. A bedroom is on the right, with a Dutch kitchen in back. In the fireplace of the latter a memorial fire burns; it was lighted from a flame sent from Pittsburgh before her death by the aged daughter of the

207

composer. Across the back of the house is a broad porch looking down upon a vista of parkland, bordering a fresh-water lagoon that was named by Mr. Ford the "Suwanee River."

At its original site the house stood on the side of a slope, with living quarters downstairs and bedrooms above. The lower floor has been changed into a basement housing the heating apparatus.

Outside on the lawn is an attractive doghouse, the home of "Old Dog Tray." In the waters of the lagoon is a stern-wheeler, the *Suwanee,* named after a river boat in which Edison often traveled a Florida stream near Fort Myers during his winter visits. After the original boat had sunk, its engines were raised and installed on the new *Suwanee* in Greenfield Village.

Chronologically speaking, the oldest home in the Village is the Cotswold Cottage at the end of the lane. In seeking to trace the development of the American home, Mr. Ford resolved to go to England for one that would illustrate that from which the early forefathers migrated

208

● Front façade of Edison Institute Museum, showing replica of Independence Hall.

● The Edison Institute Museum—Transportation Section.

to New England shores. He selected a shepherd's home in the Cotswold hills.

The feat of bringing across the Atlantic a 500-ton house and putting it up again, stone by stone, was not an easy task. Yet within six months fires were again burning placidly on its blackened hearths, and the workmen who came to reconstruct it were on their way back to England from Dearborn.

The cottage has been furnished in the early seventeenth century period: with wooden trenchers and Delft ware on the ancient tables as in its original setting three centuries ago.

In keeping with the simple, rugged habits of the shepherds who once lived here, the furniture is sturdy, constructed of stout oak with severe lines. The fireside settle dates back to the time of Charles I. On top of a side table rests a Bible chest with the bun feet so popular at the beginning of that century. Lighting methods of the time are illustrated by several different forms, rush lamp, Betty lamp, and candle holder. In front of one hearth is a kidney spit for roasting meat. A pot hook hangs on a chain, less convenient than the crane.

209

The dropleaf table in this room is put together with wooden pegs; its legs have the spiral twist popular in the Jacobean period.

The Edison homestead from Ontario has an unusual historical background. When William Lyon McKenzie rebelled against the Tory government in 1837, Samuel Edison, an innkeeper of Vienna, sided with him, and a price was placed on his head. While soldiers were ransacking the homestead, he fled across the winter snow to the American boundary, crossing the St. Clair River on the ice. After wandering along the border as far south as Ohio, he settled in Milan, brought wife and family across Lake Erie, and on February 11, 1847, gave to the world his son, Thomas Alva Edison.

There are other homes in the Village besides those along the shaded lane. In the rear of the General Store are two from early Michigan.

One of these is a log cabin that originally stood near the boyhood home of Henry Ford, and was the abode of a hermit and naturalist. Often the young farm boy visited him, and occasionally spent the night in the attic. In its

210

rear are an outdoor brick oven, and an upright hollow log such as was used in pioneer days for smoking meats.

Alongside the cabin is a small white dwelling typical of a century ago in Michigan, named the Gardner House. Two rooms comprise the downstairs, one a kitchen and dining-room, the other a bedroom. They are separated by a central fireplace. The house stands in the Village in the same relative position to the Scotch Settlement School as it did seven decades ago, when the youthful Henry Ford lived in the neighborhood.

Chapter IX

INDUSTRY AND AGRICULTURE

I

CLOSELY ALLIED

with the growth of the Edison Institute has been the development of a closer link between the manufacturer and the farmer. Experiments seeking a product that could be grown on the farm and utilized in industry were begun by young men from Wayside Inn when they moved into the laboratory set up for their use in Greenfield Village in 1929.

"I believe," said Mr. Ford, "that Industry and Agriculture are natural partners. Agriculture suffers from lack of a market for its product, Industry suffers from lack of employment for its surplus men. Bringing them together heals the ailments of both. I see the time coming when the farmer not only will raise raw materials for industry, but will do the

215

initial processing on his farm. He will stand on both feet—one foot on the soil for his livelihood, the other in industry for the cash he needs. Then he will have a double security."

Symbolizing his ideas, the spade of Luther Burbank, greatest of plant experimenters, was imbedded in the wet cement of the Museum cornerstone by Edison. Food values were studied in a diet laboratory in the rear of the Engineering Laboratory, while the young men in the "Chemical Plant" sought oils, proteins, carbohydrates and fibers of value to industry.

Several tons of wheat, thousands of bushels of carrots, sunflowers, cabbages, onions and cornstalks were experimented with.

During the winter of 1930 Edison visited them and inscribed a message in pencil, which they framed and hung in their laboratory:

> Experiment, and Nature will talk to you.
> Don't experiment with lead-pencils.

Reporting on their progress at the second Edison birthday luncheon in 1931, the young man in charge said:

"We have gradually enlarged our goal until

216

now it is our purpose to 'industrialize agriculture.' By that is meant, we are going to take the produce from the soil, separate the part that has food value, make it into a perfect food for man, and then take the rest of the plant and find a use for it. It will make that farm a real productive unit, and the full use of the soil will be obtained.

"To accomplish this, the boys are going at it from several angles. For instance, one is working on the food end. He is finding the reactions that take place inside the body, to see just what food is really beneficial. To help in determining the proper diet we have some young pigs that will be fed and observed.

"Another line of attack is the raising of food, and that means fertilizing, and so forth. One young man, who has conducted experiments along this line, has some very promising results. In fact, a greenhouse is to be erected whereby these tests can be carried down to the last degree.

"The materials that are wasted now, like stalks and straw garbage, are being made to yield valuable products, such as fibers, gas and

217

fertilizers, the rest of the boys being engaged on these problems."

Late that year Mr. Ford and the young man felt they were approaching solution of their problem with a plant common to Manchukuo, the soybean. Not only is it a highly nutritious food for the table or as forage, but it builds up the soil by bringing nitrogen into it, and, best of all, it contains oil and other products of definite value in industry.

In the vicinity of Dearborn and adjoining counties, Mr. Ford had twenty thousand acres available for planting of experimental farm products. Within two years more than 7,400 acres devoted to soybeans. About $1,250,000 was expended in experimenting with the legume by the Ford company.

As the acreage in Lenawee and Washtenaw counties began yielding, he proposed to restore the district schools and to set old mills whirring once more.

"I foresee the time," he said, "when Industry shall no longer denude the forests which require generations to mature, nor use up the mines which were ages in making, but shall

218

draw its material largely from the annual produce of the fields.

"When that day comes, and it is surely on the way, the farmer will not lack a market, and the worker will not lack a job. More people will live in the country. The present unnatural condition will be naturally balanced again. Our foundations will once more be securely laid in the land.

"The day of small industry near farms will return, because much of the material grown for industry can be given its first processing by men who raised it. The master farmer will become, as he was in former years, master of a form of Industry besides.

"Our times are primitive. True progress is yet to come. The industrial age has scarcely dawned as yet; we see only its first crude beginnings."

II

No claim has been advanced that the Edison Institute or Mr. Ford originated soybean research in America. The United States government itself has taken interest in the matter and

219

established several laboratories throughout the country. The plant was introduced to this continent early in the nineteenth century, merely as a curiosity. Actual cultivation to any extent came in the last quarter of the century.

Of the 4,000 varieties known, about 150 have been grown successfully here, although only ten or fifteen are used widely. When experiments were commenced by the company, about 300 were tested, and finally a new type was developed. It was named "The Greenfield."

The reasons for the choice of the soybean from among the farm products tried out have been briefly mentioned. Coupled with them is the fact that it is a hardy plant, able to mature in excessively dry or excessively wet weather.

The plant requires little cultivation—just enough to give it a start up to six inches' height and thereafter only enough to control the weeds. On the Ford farms, the plants were cultivated with tractors along rows twenty-eight inches apart. The stalks usually grow about four to four and one-half feet high.

Another big advantage to the farmer is that

220

soybeans do not need to be harvested when other crops press him. The vines stand up straight and stiff—except on certain types of heavy soil. Their leaves fall off at frost and the pods remain. The crop may be harvested any time during the winter, enabling the farmer to employ his time profitably during the months when work is lightest. Indeed, some of the Ford crops have been harvested in sub-zero weather in December. Some record plants have yielded as high as 300 pods.

In order to stimulate interest among the farmers of Michigan, Mr. Ford arranged to provide them gratis with soybean seed. This was issued to them as desired, with the agreement that when the harvest was in, an equal amount of seed would be returned.

Spaces precludes more than a brief résumé of the many experiments conducted with the different varieties. For industrial purposes, that with the most oil content was desirable, while in the development of food products, the bean's taste was the first consideration.

Nor did the experimenting along this line cease when success was met. Experimental

221

tracts of the beans were encountered by motorists driving along roads near Dearborn as late as 1937. One of the tests was with various ores in the soil to determine their effect on the bean, for even a minute quantity of metal in the residue would add to the strength of the plastic.

One of the first by-products to be extracted from the soybean was the oil. After much experimenting, in which simplicity of operation was a prime factor, a process was evolved whereby about 400 pounds could be obtained from a ton of beans. Whereas some methods left something like 30 percent of the oil in this residue, the one they perfected averaged about 95 percent.

The principal use of the oil was in the exterior finish of the car. Ford chemists developed an enamel, a principal ingredient of which came from the farmer's field. The oil was used both in the production of the glycerine used in making glyptol resin and as the oil modifier of the finished enamel. In a single year more than a million and a quarter gallons were consumed.

Not only was this use developed, but it was

222

found that the enamel was superior in every respect to lacquer, from the original gloss to its complete resistance to deterioration. It cost less by the gallon, required less on the job, and saved tremendously in labor. About fifteen pounds of oil was used in finishing each car, and the only reason all Ford cars were not thus finished was that there was not enough oil-crushing equipment available to produce enough.

Another use for it was discovered in the foundry, when the chemists proved that it was quite as effective as linseed-oil in mixing with sand to make foundry cores. The core-makers used it as a bond after the core was baked. Nearly another quarter-million gallons a year went into this service.

Soft soaps and paints provided another outlet. When Mr. Ford and Edsel Ford arranged to exhibit at the Chicago World's Fair in 1934, their building was painted entirely with paint containing soybean oil as the only drying oil.

Meanwhile experimenting was not discontinued in other agricultural products. Visitors who entered the Village in 1933 found spread

223

before them a garden in which plants varying from the castor-oil bean to cotton and tobacco were being grown.

Oil was made from canteloupe and watermelon seeds; pulp from sugar beets. Grain straws, cornstalks and sugarcane pulp yielded a felted material on the general order of paper, sufficiently strong for several uses in an automobile body. It could be pressed, coated and formed so as to fit exactly in any desired place. It was weatherproof, mold proof, and termite-proof.

As Mr. Ford told a writer from the *Rotarian* magazine (Arthus Van Vlissinger, Jr.) : "No matter what we may guess as to the proportion of automobile parts that can be built from the fruit of the field, our guess will fall far short of the eventual result."

III

When Mr. Ford announced that he proposed to include, as an important part of the company's exhibit at the Chicago World's Fair, an old barn, some of his associates were at first

224

● A craft shop in the museum. Old New Hampshire barber-shop, with swan-arm chair and individual mugs.

● Fire engine "Deluge" in shed. Greenfield Village.

● Century-old gristmill restored and placed in productive activity.

puzzled. The magnificent exposition with its palaces of white stone and steel seemed hardly the place for an old hay barn. But as he disclosed his purpose, it was recognized that no better way could have been chosen to fulfil it.

"What I want to show," he said, "is that any farmer who is so minded may begin on a scale within his means the partial industrialization of his farm, and the manufacture of products directly for industrial markets."

He proposed to install in the barn simple, economical apparatus such as almost any farmer could prepare for the processing of the soybean.

"There are many barns about the countryside not in use," he continued. "The plant I have in mind could be built from odds and ends. One man can run it, or a group of farmers might own it, according to the acreage planted to soybeans.

"The system we propose will not only get a complete extraction of the oil, but will have a residue that may form an excellent food for man. It is 50 percent protein and 95 percent digestible. The farmer also may feed it to his

225

livestock with excellent results. Or he may put it into another simple machine and from it manufacture plastics. Some day chairs, desks, doors and other things now made of wood will be made from soybeans or similar materials."

The barn stood originally across the road from the Ford homestead in Dearborn, where it had been built in 1863, the year of Mr. Ford's birth. For seventy years it had been used as a hay barn.

Board by board, shingle by shingle, it was taken apart, transported to the Chicago Fair grounds, and set up. Outside its doors a small tract of ground was prepared and planted to soybeans.

Within the barn simple machinery—much of it standard piping—was installed to demonstrate the processes of oil distillation and making of plastics. The first of these might be described briefly as follows:

After threshing, the soybeans are spread on the upper floor of the barn where the heat rising from below helps to dry them. Directly under an opening in the floor is a set of rollers, so placed that the beans feed into them by

226

gravity. The rollers flatten the beans into thin flakes before they pass into the extractor.

This is a pipe fixed at a 10-degree angle to the floor and filled with a solvent, generally a high-class gasoline. The flakes are fed into the bottom of the pipe and carried by a screw conveyor to the top. As the thin flakes work upward against a constant stream of gasoline, practically all the oil is removed and mixed with it.

The flakes, arriving at the top of the screw in the form of meal, leave the solvent chamber and drop into a steamer where the solvent is vaporized and driven off by a current of steam. When it leaves the steamer, the meal is granular in form and lacks even a trace of the solvent odor.

Meanwhile the gasoline, fed in at the top of the pipe, has worked its way down against the meal along the flanges of the screw, carrying the oil with it. At the bottom of the pipe, atmospheric pressure forces it into an upright piece from which it overflows, carrying all the soybean oil with it.

Distillation then turns the gasoline into a

227

vapor which rises, passes through a cooling apparatus, is condensed back into the form of gasoline and flows into the top of the pipe, or solvent chamber. It is now ready to repeat the same process, going through it over and over again.

There is nothing especially complicated about the distilling apparatus. When the gasoline flows from the bottom of the extractor it goes through a filter which removes all particles of meal. It is then run into a still, a 12-inch pipe sixteen feet long, of which the upper ten feet are filled with coke. As the solution flows over the coke it meets a rising current of live steam which drives off the solvent, leaving only the pure soybean oil at the bottom of the still.

Although the foregoing description may seem complicated, demonstrators at the barn informed visitors that the materials of which it had been constructed could be obtained almost anywhere. Only a simple welding operation was required to add the feed spout and the steaming section, capable of being performed in a small shop.

228

The only items in the plant that could not be made in town were certain pipe fittings and accessories, and the crushing rollers, which would have to be purchased. It was pointed out that when a group of farmers combined to erect such a plant, they could store two or three weeks' supply of beans at a time on the top floors and allow them to dry, thus saving the expense of a grain drier. When these had been used, a new supply could be brought in, since the soybeans could be harvested at any time during the winter.

It was also suggested that the power be self-contained. The unit displayed comprised small boiler and steam engine; even the electric lights were supplied current from a belt-driven dynamo beside the engine. Coal or wood could be used as fuel, as well as gas.

The plant was not presented as the final solution to the farm factory. Even as the World's Fair opened, Ford Motor Company engineers were seeking to make the plant more simple and economical.

In addition to demonstrating the oil extraction machinery to the farmer, the barn contained special machines that had been built to utilize the meal in car manufacture. Because of its high protein content, making it somewhat like animal horn or milk casein, experimenters of the Institute investigated its possibilities in molded products.

In time the meal was being used in making such parts of the automobile as the horn button, the gear shift lever ball, the light switch handle, the distributor base, and cover, window trim strips, and other products.

While the processes of manufacture are too technical to warrant description here, it might be said that the plastic material developed by the chemists was found to mold very solidly under pressure, and could be finished smoothly, being capable of taking a high polish. Many colors and pleasing effects could be obtained.

The development of plastic material was followed by the erection of a building 400 feet long in the Rouge plant where production could be undertaken on a commercial basis. Space for about 400 molding machines was provided here, as well as for equipment to produce 80,000 pounds of the molding material each

230

day. The construction of this new unit at a cost of approximately four million dollars was Mr. Ford's answer to the question of the permanence of the new process and products.

The cost of one pound of soybean molding material has as yet proved higher than that of a pound of steel, but the polishing and finishing of the steel makes the cost of its finished part somewhat greater than that of the finished plastic. When a molded plastic part replaces one of steel, weight is decreased with consequent reduction in gasoline consumption.

IV

Two years before experiments with the soybean in its relation to industry were commenced, the bean was the subject of another definite line of research in the food and diet laboratory maintained by the Company in the rear of the Engineering Laboratory directed by Mr. Ford's old seatmate, Dr. Edsel Ruddiman. Its purpose was to demonstrate some of the almost amazing values of the legume from the human food standpoint.

231

Among these is the fact that while it is cheap, it is also nearly complete, sufficiently so to sustain life for a long time. The 35 percent to 40 percent protein content, in a cooked condition, is as easily digested as that from any other source. All of the amino acids necessary to life are included in it, and on the other hand, it contains little or no starch. Also it has a comparatively large percentage of alkaline salts.

Many will doubtless recall the howl of laughter that went up when Mr. Ford informed a reporter one day of his belief that synthetic milk could be produced. Nevertheless, milk has been produced from the soybean in the Ford laboratories and elsewhere. It is even better than cows' milk for certain infants' cases, where skin afflictions make use of the latter undesirable. In cooking where recipes call for milk, it makes a satisfactory substitute.

When Dr. Victor Heiser, author of "An American Doctor's Odyssey," visited Greenfield Village he told me of the wide use of soybean milk among the Filipinos, and how the addition of a little oil of banana had made it much more palatable.

232

The process of manufacture is simple. After soaking the beans overnight and grinding them up fine with water (about one pound to a gallon) straining it through a cloth and heating it in a double-boiler for not more than half an hour, the milk is obtained. A little salt and sweetening are all that are required.

With this milk soybean cheese, similar to cottage cheese except in flavor, may be made. While somewhat insipid in taste, the cheese proves very useful when mixed in salads, sandwich spreads, croquettes with a food having a strong flavor.

The whole bean has many food uses, among them soups, baked beans, salads, and canning. As the flavor of the soya is slightly stronger than that of the ordinary bean, onions and tomatoes are often used to cover it.

The process of canning the green soybean was first demonstrated under Dr. Ruddiman's direction. Production of soybeans in 1935 totaled 590 cans; and in 1936 it reached 1,000. The canned green bean could be served on the table much as one would serve peas or lima-beans.

233

As in the industrial field, extraction of the oil from the soybeans is a necessary preliminary to many uses to which it can then be adapted. Indeed, the oil itself has a definite value in cooking, or as a table or salad oil.

After the extraction, one of the most important products is flour. The beans are ground in a type of mill made up of sharp steel revolving surfaces, and the product, a pure flour from the bean without mixture with any other substance, finds a ready market among visitors at the Village. It is used in many common baked goods such as bread, rolls, muffins, biscuits, cakes, cookies, and so on, and has been found to give best results when mixed with a percentage of wheat flour.

Another product that has proved popular with visitors is the salted soya, put up in small packages like nuts. In preparing these, the bean is soaked in water for a time, then roasted in hot soya oil. The salt is added to taste.

One of the most valuable properties of the bean is Lecithem, found in the human brain and in almost every cell of the human body. It is contained in the bean to the extent of one to

234

three percent. Not much has been done, as yet, with this compound of fat and protein, except in the making of chocolate sauce and coating for soybean candies, with which the Ford men have done much experimenting.

As a practical demonstration of the possibilities of the soybean in a variety of foods, a dinner was served one August evening in 1934 at the Ford exhibit in the Chicago Century of Progress Fair. Every dish on the menu was comprised, in part at least, of the legume.

Following was the list:

Tomato Juice Seasoned with Soybean Sauce
Salted Soybeans   Celery Stuffed with Soybean Cheese
Purée of Soybean   Soybean Crackers
Soybean Croquettes with Tomato Sauce
Buttered Green Soybeans
Pineapple Ring with Soybean Cheese
and Soybean Dressing
Soybean Bread with Soybean Butter
Apple Pie (Soybean Crust)
Cocoa with Soybean Milk   Soybean Coffee
Assorted Soybean Cookies   Soybean Cakes
Assorted Soybean Candy

Chapter X

LITTLE FACTORIES

I

*H*AND IN HAND WITH
the development of uses for agricultural products in industry, and in the restoring of the
countryside with its district schools and lovely
old houses, has gone the revival of little factories along small streams, providing part-time
incomes for the men who raise the crops.

This idea had been in Mr. Ford's mind for
many years. When America was emerging
from the World War, and automobile plants
were being returned to their owners by the
government, Mr. Ford told Upton Sinclair: *

"I have bought a lot of little water-power
sites in Michigan, and at each one of these little
sites we are making some one part of the tractor. We do the work in the winter-time when

* *Reconstruction*, May, 1919.

239

the farmers in the locality have nothing to do. We make enough parts to last us over the summer, and in that way we don't have to bring in outside labor, but we build up the neighborhood. That is my idea of industry; a lot of little centers."

Since then Mr. Ford's idea has become strengthened; in fact, during the past ten years he has doubled the number of his little factories in rural districts. Some are in the heart of the soybean farm area, and eventually will be assigned to production operations involving the legume. All are on small rivers, usually occupying a site where once a dam and waterwheel powered a pioneer mill.

At the outset six village industries, five on the Rouge and one on the Huron River, all within twenty miles of Dearborn, were started, employing men of the vicinity. The overhead cost was found to be less than in a big factory, and the men, with their opportunity to till land in the growing season, had a security not possessed by their less fortunate city brothers. They had every advantage the city could offer, for their automobiles could take them quickly

240

back and forth. Their children's schooling was of the best. Their homes could be operated far more cheaply than would be possible in the city, yet their earnings were proportionately as much as those of the city worker.

The first of these village plants was opened in the town of Northville in 1920, when Mr. Ford acquired a small brick factory that for more than a score of years had manufactured fence posts, screen doors, wheelbarrows and ship tackle in that picturesque rural community on the Rouge River. After it closed its doors, he purchased the building and moved into it machinery from his Highland Park plant for the production of valves.

At first, experienced workmen from the city plant operated it, but as time went on men from the village and countryside were put to work at regular Ford wages. Today, nearly all of the 400 employes are nearby residents, living on small tracts of two or three acres. The rough castings for the parts were brought from the city foundry by truck, machined, finished and tested, then shipped back to motor assembly.

The question has been asked: Is not this

241

movement of material expensive? Isn't it costly to set up small plants for work formerly carried on under one roof? The Ford experience has not found it so. The cost of transportation is low, and the enthusiasm of the workmen has resulted in a superior product more efficiently produced.

During the sixteen years of its operation, this little village factory produced more than 181,000,000 valves.

II

One of the predominating features of the Ford small plants has been their architectural attractiveness. Invariably the grounds are land-scaped, lawns, shrubs, shade-trees and hedges are cared for throughout the year, and both exterior and interior are maintained at the height of cleanliness. Usually beside the plants an artificial lake is created by the dam, and a public park results.

In the olden days, gristmills, sawmills, foun-dries and small industries lined the meandering shores of the Rouge River, and utilized its water

242

power. With the growth of large cities and gathering of population in congested centers, these plants gradually ceased to function and went out of business.

One of the oldest was a tall wooden building that stood on the Ann Arbor trail near the settlement of Nankin Mills. Originally a gristmill, it had been framed of massive hand-hewn beams and finished in clapboards. When Mr. Ford acquired it he rehabilitated it, painted it white in the colonial manner, and constructed a headrace to carry the Rouge water to a modern turbine-driven electric generator.

Employment for about nine of the neighboring farmers was provided at first in the manufacture of machine screws and later in dies and engravings. When the plant was retooled to undertake the new production, forty more men were added to the force, and an entire department was transferred from the Rouge plant into the country. The machine screw work went elsewhere.

Here the men were able to work under ideal conditions; on the hot summer days, fresh country breezes wafted in through open windows.

243

Outside in elms, birds sang all day long to the hum of the busy machines. To make their lot more enjoyable, Mr. Ford erected a brick schoolhouse nearby where the workers' children might receive the same schooling benefits as at other Ford schools. The reader will recall this as the last of the rural schools opened by the Institute in 1937.

Between Nankin Mills and Northville, Mr. Ford erected three little village plants, one to employ women exclusively.

At Waterford, a few miles down the Rouge from Northville, was built a two-story factory to furnish jobs for about sixty-five men in the manufacture of the measuring instruments, gauges and precision tools used throughout the various Ford enterprises. Power was obtained from an electric generator connected with a turbine driven by a 21-foot head of water.

Farther down the river, the plant to employ women was set among a grove of trees. It was planned to make generator parts here, since they require the fine touch and care that women can furnish, without requiring heavy labor. Most of the eighty or more women at work

244

here come from the countryside. Married ones are not employed unless their husbands are incapacitated, and women in those circumstances are enabled to support husband and family.

On the site of another old gristmill at the village of Plymouth, still farther down the river, Mr. Ford constructed a modern small plant to manufacture taps. Work for about thirty-five men was provided here, of such sort that a single day's production, worth several thousand dollars, could be shipped out in a fairly small package. In other respects the plant was a midget. It boasted the smallest turbo-electric generator owned by Mr. Ford, a five horsepower unit used as an auxiliary.

In addition to these tiny plants on the Rouge, a larger one was constructed under Mr. Ford's direction on a different stream, the Huron. For its site he chose the flourishing community of Flat Rock, some miles south of Dearborn at a point where the river flows under Telegraph Road, direct route between Michigan cities and Ohio. A wide dam was built here to back up the water, and at its far side a glass-walled factory was erected for the manufacture of head lamps, tail lamps, and dome lamps. More than 500 men were put to work.

III

After the establishment of the Edison Institute and successful experimenting with the soybean, came the acquiring of large acreage for agricultural purposes. The reader has heard of the manner in which the district schools through that area were at once restored. Equally if not even more important was the restoration of the old mills for productive activity once more.

First of the many additions to the list of little village factories was another on the Huron River in the City of Ypsilanti. Like most other communities, Ypsilanti had suffered during the depression and when in 1932 Mr. Ford started operations in a plant at the edge of town, the effect on the general spirit of the citizens was most wholesome.

To make sufficient power available, it was necessary to back up the river for several miles,

246

creating a wide and deep lake. Employment for nearly seven hundred men and seventy women was provided. Generators, starters, and starter switches were manufactured for both the Ford V-8 and the new Lincoln-Zephyr automobiles.

The plant was designed to form an industry complete within itself. Steel and other raw materials are brought in by railroad and truck, and thirty minutes later the completed parts are ready to leave the factory. The main building is 160 feet wide and 390 long, and is of brick and steel construction.

In former days intensified production of parts requiring highly skilled craftsmanship, such as these electrical parts, was deemed impossible. Even the machines used had to be designed and manufactured, new tests for the finished products had to be devised, and workmen had to be trained in the new method.

In the fall of 1936, twelve unemployed boys from that year's graduating classes at nearby high schools, all between the ages of eighteen and nineteen, were brought into the Ypsilanti plant to become apprentices. They had been

247

selected carefully by their teachers on the basis
of scholarship, aptitude and interest in me-
chanics. By talking with the older men and by
observation, they were allowed to choose the
department in which they would receive instruction. If this proved to be different from
what had been expected, they made a new
choice.

The period of training and study lasted for
three months, during which they received pay
at the rate of fifty-five cents an hour. As soon
as they completed the course they went to work
on the regular minimum wage of six dollars a
day. Their places in the plant school were
taken by twelve more boys. The process has
continued in force ever since.

The majority of men employed in this plant
were also home gardeners, some of them tilling
several acres of ground. Twenty-five of those
given work here were between the ages of sixty
and seventy-seven.

Some of the richest soil in Michigan lies in
the Huron Valley, and for years was used by
truck gardeners supplying the Detroit market.
Approximately 4,000 acres of those lands are

248

owned by the company and made available to workers for spare time gardens.

As Mr. Ford said: "No unemployment insurance can be compared to an alliance between a man and a plot of land. With one foot in industry and another foot in the land, human society is firmly balanced against most economic uncertainties. With a job to supply him with cash, and a plot of land to guarantee him support, the individual is doubly secure. Stocks may fail, but seed time and harvest do not fail."

Four miles below the Ypsilanti plant is a wide earthen dam 1,100 feet long, surmounted by a paved highway. Above the dam spreads the artificial lake 1,200 acres in area over the wide bottom lands that stretch away from the original banks of the Huron River. The thirty-three-foot water head at the dam is capable of producing 2,800 horsepower. The total output of the two turbine generators, 2,100 kilowatts, is used by the plant.

While this factory was being set up and placed in operation, several more were being planned, notably in the soybean area. Mr. Ford's activities embraced now the Raisin and

249

Saline Rivers as well as the Huron and the Rouge.

Along the last-named stream two important developments occurred. The time had come to replace the old ungainly brick factory at Northville, earliest of the village industries, with a one-story, thoroughly up-to-date plant. A handsome modern edifice of brick and steel was erected, with more floor space than heretofore, and opportunity to employ additional men. More than one-third as many machines as in the old plant were installed. Under the new set-up the men were able to turn out as many valves in sixteen hours as had previously required twenty-four. An overshot wheel operated by water piped under the broad lawn from the head of a small city pond, added a reminiscent touch to the building. The new plant was completed in 1936.

Last of the little plants along this river was added midway between those at Plymouth and Nankin Mills. At the end of a pretty, winding lake created by water backed up by its dam, it provided employment for about fifteen men. Twist drills were manufactured. Newburg

250

close by was a sleepy village dreaming of past
glories till the modern Ford factory was set up
in its midst. A paved parkway drive along the
edge of the lake was completed a few years ago
by the county road commissioners, with picnic
stoves, tables and benches, play fields, rest
houses and athletic grounds.

IV

Before the year 1937 had closed, several more
small industrial plants had been completed or
restored and in some cases were in operation
or in process of getting ready. One of the first
of these was at Dundee, a rural community on
the Raisin River southeast of the Lenawee
County acreage and located about fifty miles
· from Dearborn.

Years ago the plant was known as the Davis
gristmill, and drew its power from a dam and
water-wheel. Mr. Ford's workmen rebuilt the
dam, headworks and draft tube, and the reju-
venated system with its hydro-electric installa-
tion was capable of producing 150 horsepower.
A powerhouse was erected adjoining the rear

251

of the restored mill, out of stone dug from the bed when the mill race was enlarged. Another problem here was the straightening of the river in the adjacent territory to care for the excess spill.

Employment for forty men was provided in the village, inaugurating an important, almost revolutionary improvement in the spirit and prospects of the entire population. The output comprised welding electrodes such as are used in departments in all Ford plants. A group of Dundee high school graduates were brought into the plant as apprentices, much as at Ypsilanti.

In the heart of the soybean country, in Tecumseh, center of several Institute rural school projects, an old mill foundation was located by his workmen, the remains of a gristmill that had been erected in 1825 to grind the wheat of the early settlers. The mill itself was later destroyed by fire. Exactly one century later, water poured once more over a huge waterwheel that turned beside the Hayden Mills, restored by Mr. Ford. It was turned on by the great-great-grandson of Chief Tecumseh for

252

whom that town had been named. The occasion was made a community celebration. A banquet was held during the evening, and a bust of the Shawnee chief was unveiled.

After its restoration, this mill was used for cleaning and sacking soybeans for seed, preparing them for distribution to neighboring farmers in the spring.

Two other old mills were restored, one in the back country at Sharon Hollow not far from the town of Manchester; the other at the village of Saline where the Chicago pike crosses the Saline River a few miles north of the soybean farms. The original Shuyler mill was built here between 1840 and 1845, obtaining its power from a dam and water-wheel. In later years the dam was washed away, and when Mr. Ford's engineers prepared for the restoration, they decided to locate it downstream to create a larger reserve supply of water.

The fall of 1936 also found workmen busy at the town of Milan east of the soybean area, and at Milford on the upper reaches of the Huron, preparing for more little plants. Other power sites meanwhile were acquired by Mr. Ford for possible use at a later time.

v

To climax his recent program, Mr. Ford during 1936 undertook the construction of a model farm—industrial community deep in the virgin hardwood forests of Upper Michigan, not far from the spot where he has gone for a brief respite during the hot season. The site chosen was ten miles south of Keweenaw Bay of Lake Superior, on the banks of a trout stream, Plumbago Creek. It was named "Alberta."

Two years previous the spot was wild timberland pierced by a highway. First, the highway was moved to skirt the proposed town. Little Plumbago Creek was damned to form a crystal-clear fifty-acre lake at one end of the valley. Below the dam was erected the principal industrial unit of the village, a modern, compact sawmill housed in a spotlessly white clapboard building, surrounded by wide landscaped lawn.

Across the old highway from the mill, now the main village artery, is a completely land-

254

scaped residential section. There stand a dozen modern homes on roads stretching back to the foot of the wooded slopes. Clean and inviting with stone and white clapboard sides outlined against the green forest background, their attractiveness is one of which any community might well boast.

Lumber is the backbone of Alberta. Significant is the fact that Alberta, with its industrial life wholly dependent on the cutting of lumber, faces a future of security. In the conservation of these northern timberlands is found the reason.

This new project is centered in a six-square-mile area of solid hardwood which it alone may draw upon for support. All logging in the area will be done on what is termed in lumbering industry a "selective basis." The quantity of wood cut throughout the years will be constant, thus employment in the mill will not vary.

Selective logging is a form of conservation relatively new. Many forestry experts look upon it more enthusiastically than they do upon reforestation. Under this plan, only those

255

trees are generally cut which have reached or are near full maturity. There are, of course, exceptions. Many trees are found in forests which, though they should still have years of growth ahead of them, are doomed to an early death. Insects and disease have attacked them.

To leave them standing would mean losing what good wood still remains in them. It would also mean that growth adjacent would be exposed to disease. To the experienced eye of the forester, stands of timber are recognizable which will never mature in the face of vicissitudes of nature—deterioration of soil, or the failure of proper windbreak. To leave the trees might mean losing them altogether through decay or death, or later finding it impractical to remove at all because of the prohibitive cost of lumbering when only a few scattered trees are cut at a time.

When a forest is properly thinned, timber will grow remarkably faster than under normal conditions. It will reach maturity in a rate of time which permits the lumberman to plan his timber cutting over a long range as the farmer plans his crop plantings. Thus by cutting the

256

Alberta reserve at a predetermined rate on a selective basis, the village sawmill should never be without reserve timber. By the time all available timber has been cut in the last areas more trees will have matured in the areas first logged years before.

When ground was broken for the Alberta sawmill in the spring of 1936, the clearing of 350 acres of timberland, enough space for a village of three-score homes and community buildings, was also commenced. On September 1, 1936, the twang of a band saw biting wood first reechoed against the timber-covered slopes rising around Alberta. Eight hours a day, five days every Ford work week since, the band saw at Alberta has been humming a song of activity.

The little mill is able to cut around 15,000 feet of lumber in the regular Ford eight-hour workday. Compared with most commercial mills it is almost miniature. Three other Ford sawmills in upper Michigan each cut from twenty to fifty times as many board feet of lumber in the same number of hours. But the little mill is compact, modern and complete in every detail. It is fully capable of supporting

257

the community being built around it, as its size was predetermined by the amount of timber that could be selectively cut from the forest lands consigned to it alone.

Behind the thin column of listless white smoke curving from the tall stack above the mill powerhouse is a little story of industrial ingenuity. Never need fuel be brought to Alberta for firing the 125-pound steam pressure Titusville locomotive boiler. All the slashing, sawdust and scrap left at the band saw, the edger and trimmer in the mill, are automatically carried to storage bins to be fed to the furnace as needed.

Conveyors, like those in big factories, draw logs up out of the pond and into the mill, carry wood through the mill in every stage of lumber production and then automatically load finished lumber on trucks for shipment out of Alberta. Power for this system is provided by a 25-horsepower steam engine. A 70-horsepower steam engine powers the thirty-one-foot band saw and other mill machinery.

"How can Alberta be certain of a continued demand for its lumber?" The fact that prob-

258

ably as long as the Ford Motor Company builds cars and trucks, wood will be needed, is the answer. Even though all the wood in one 1937 Ford V-8 amounted to only about five board feet (mostly for seat frames), last year lumber requirements in Ford industries drew from the company's timber holding in Upper Michigan a total of more than 120,000,000 feet of lumber.

Equally important as prosperous industry to a substantial community are attractive homes and homesites. Unlike the typical sprawling, ragged lumber town, the residential section of Alberta is outstanding in its attractiveness. Each of the dozen new homes already completed is located on a lot 90 feet wide and 150 feet deep. No two of the new one- and two-story homes is alike in shape or design. Each has a distinctive individuality which is pleasing in itself. Varying in cubical content from 15,000 to 24,000 feet, they are modern to the minute in every detail. Exteriors are white clapboard and their full basement foundations are of native fieldstone. Each home is completely insulated and boasts attractively painted plaster walls, maple floors, birch woodwork trim and fire-resisting roofing.

The built-in features include modern baths, metal bathroom cupboards and fixtures, large-sized kitchen sinks with spacious drain board, hot air heat, electricity and lighting fixtures appropriate to the interior color schemes.

A thousand feet from the residential section, high on the side of one of the slopes, clear, cool water from a nearby woodland spring is gathered in a reservoir with a 100-foot head. This water reserve is ample for many more than the three-score homes already planned for the village.

When children of the mill workers troop off to school they don't carry lunches, for they haven't far to go. Two new frame and field-stone schoolhouses reminiscent of half a century ago have already taken their places in the residential section. As in the other Institute schools, classes are not limited to academic study. Children are taught to do and make things with their hands. Girls study the various phases of home economics; boys are given an opportunity to watch skilled craftsmen work

260

and learn the rudiments of trades that may later be of benefit to them.

A true agro-industrial community, Alberta is founded on this principle of the double security of farm and factory. Each family will be provided as much land as they require for gardens, with which they can supplement their cash income from the mill paid at the regular Ford wage scale.

Even as the residential section of the community was still under construction during the summer of 1937, and while land was still being cleared and graded, hundreds of tourists visited the project daily. Stopping at the village they watched, many of them for the first time, production of lumber from big logs. Visitors saw a new community spring up in the wilderness, and heard the interesting story of its principle and background.

Visitors to Alberta in 1938 will find a wooded park beside the dammed waters of Plumbago Creek. Cook stoves, tables, cool spring water and rest rooms will beckon them to linger at this new northern Michigan beauty spot.

Chapter XI

CONCLUSION

I

*A*LTHOUGH HE HAS
rounded three-quarters of a century, Mr. Ford
has the physical agility and mental alertness of
a man many years younger. His movements
are nervous and rapid. He does not seem to
tire easily. One reason for this is his fondness
for certain forms of recreational exercise, like
riding a bicycle or dancing the old-time steps.
Those familiar with such numbers as the "Little Old Log Cabin in the Lane" know that they
provide exercise as well as fun and grace. No
dancer on the ballroom floor whether old or
young enjoys them more thoroughly, participates more eagerly, or dances more gracefully,
than does he himself.

His hours are long and fully occupied, yet he
seems to be able to dismiss his responsibilities

from his mind, hoist his feet to an easy position on the edge of a desk, and relax completely. While he has an office, it is the last place in the world you are likely to find him. He is on the go between Village, schools, laboratory, Museum, farm and factory, and sooner or later, if an employe is engaged on work requiring Mr. Ford's attention, he is sure to drop in and see what progress is being made. Many key men he sees once or twice every day. He is capable of swift decisions, and just as capable of deferring a matter for weeks or months if he is not ready yet to reach a decision. Delays mean nothing to him if he sees that by going slowly, better results may be obtained. Once he had decided a question, speedy and efficient action must follow.

Never one to coddle those who work for him, he is a firm believer that capable executives will make themselves, just as large stones rise to the top of a barrel when it is shaken. He has a place and work for each one who rises, but first of all the man must emerge. Likely as not, when he has an important mission to despatch or a difficult job to accomplish, he

266

will select a man who has demonstrated fitness and ability to get results in an entirely different field. His organization is so large that he can fill almost any need that develops, from playing a cymbalum to training an operatic chorus. Indeed, experienced men for both these jobs were found when needed.

As a result, working for him is a constant challenge to develop toward more efficient performance. He himself is the best teacher, and those closest to him profit from that association in character and strength, often without realizing it. He permits no one to become self-satisfied or to stagnate, unless one insists upon it. The human equation is far more important to him than the material. Viewing his responsibility as he does—namely the providing of work for the benefit of his fellow-men—it could not be otherwise.

The question is sometimes asked: What will happen to the Edison Institute when the day comes that Mr. Ford no longer takes an active part in its direction?

That question never occurs to those who are engaged in it with him, because all of their efforts and attention are concentrated on the present. That is how Mr. Ford would have it. He himself has no worries for the future. As mentioned before, that is one thing that does not concern him.

But to those individuals who make the inquiry because of their own deep interest in the project and their hope that it will be continued for generations to come, here is an answer: Every thought and plan that has gone into the project has been based on the determination that it shall stand in the future as an inspiration to young America to go forward.

THE END